teachers to his contemporaries, Péguy, Bernanos, Charles Du Bos, Max Jacob, Simone Weil, Claudel, all of whom have preceded him into eternity. He recalls with chagrin that period of his youth when he, along with other brilliant writers and artists, succumbed to the recklessness that followed the 1918 Armistice and fell victim to the antic charm of Jean Cocteau. Mauriac can be hard on himself. And in his appraisals of his agnostic contemporaries, or of slightly younger men such as Aragon, Sartre, Malraux, he does not allow his religious beliefs to cloud his judgment of them.

We are admitted, through these pages, to the intimate company of François Mauriac, to share with him the peaceful seclusion of Malagar, the ancient manor house near Bordeaux where he now lives in semi-retirement. We share with him his periods of serene confidence, even his moments of anguished doubt—fleeting moments, for this great writer's faith in God and mankind has been tested and proved throughout the years, over and over again.

THE INNER PRESENCE
(*Nouveaux Mémoires Intérieurs*)

THE
INNER
PRESENCE

(Nouveaux Mémoires Intérieurs)

Recollections of My Spiritual Life

By FRANCOIS MAURIAC

Translated from the French
by Herma Briffault

THE BOBBS-MERRILL COMPANY, INC.
A Subsidiary of Howard W. Sams & Co., Inc.
Publishers Indianapolis Kansas City New York

The Bobbs-Merrill Company, Inc.
A Subsidiary of Howard W. Sams & Co., Inc.
Publishers, Indianapolis   Kansas City   New York

Library of Congress catalog card number 68-11150
Printed in the United States of America

Designed by Quentin Fiore

Contents

The Inner Presence

(Nouveaux Mémoires Intérieurs)

I ─────

A Meditation on Old Age, its losses and gains

A book I intended to discuss remains open before me, but unread. I tried in vain to read it; my attention was not held. A new record has still not been played; it has not even been taken from its envelope. A certain chill is creeping over me and makes me afraid. No, it is not exactly coldness, for I do not feel detached from anything or anybody; it is merely that I seem to be losing interest in everything except the fact of being alive; from now on, this is enough to occupy my mind. My hand on my knee is still warmed by the red tides of the sea throbbing within me, but those tides will not ebb and flow eternally. My world is nearing its end, and sometimes I can think of nothing else during these last moments before the final one. This, then, is old age.

No more do I find in books the reflected image of life, and I seem to read books only when forced to do so by my calling, which is to read and then discuss what I have read. Indeed, I am now surprised that fiction, stories that are untrue or have only the truth of imitation, could ever have made me forget this real presence within me, this thinking self that will be here for only a little while longer, for how long I do not know, but certainly the time will be brief. Soon everything will end for me . . . or perhaps begin?

My own inmost thoughts interest me more than any I could find in books, and I will let nothing distract me from them. This explains what keeps me from putting the new record on the record-player. But who would have imagined that I could ever let all those voices fall silent one day by no longer using the power I have to awaken them at any time, as I used to do!

To avoid being put to shame by scandalized friends, I listen to music now and then and do some reading—in other words, I continue to do what I have been doing for years; I remain faithful to the daily cult rendered to the expression of ideas, to what we call style, which is like the particular sound of each voice. I still occasionally enjoy the rhythm of sounds, the noise, the din of tinned music dispensed by records. I open haphazardly a tin of Bach, or Mozart or Bécaud. As for the books, there they all are, the classics, ranged on their shelves against the wall. But the latest things, the newest novels that will live for a day, constantly irrupt here, like flies, lighting on chairs, rugs, everywhere except on the crowded book shelves of my study, which are infinitely more encumbered than my memory, where blows the wind of forgetfulness.

My own works are there, too; they return from foreign lands and the provinces for me to autograph, or they have been translated into an alien language. I entertain, I confess, a singular loathing for them, the aversion we have for our own reflected face, since that writing, congealed forever, cannot be revised, and is condemned, if it lives, to eternal mediocrity.

This swarm of books no longer diverts me from the fact of living. Oh, what drew me back to Malagar were not the lilacs in the garden from which I have just returned to the house, nor the spring-time, that phrase-maker, nor that terrace, nor that hornbeam tree which I dare mention again without fear that it will arouse whispering and suppressed laughter in the class . . . No, the enchantment consists in being here, on my hilltop, beside the road along which no one passes; here there are no distractions, I am shielded from any kind of entertainment, any prospect whatsoever of supposed "pleasures." Before leaving town, how delighted I was to cross out the words "will attend" on the theatre invitations, happy at the very thought of missing this or that show.

There exists for me now no other story to tell or hear except that of having been born, of having lived, and of continuing to live. What happened in the past means nothing, now. What remains, this ebb and flow of life-blood, I listen to in a profound idleness which I enjoy only here on the terrace, my head leaning against a lime-tree;

I gently stroke its mossy pelt, humming a tune, and am reminded of Maurice de Guérin who, one day, embraced a lilac bush, as he sang to himself softly. That was, I believe, in a Parisian garden, long ago, when there were still lilacs in Paris, that Paris which now overwhelms me with everything that fatigues, bewilders, and bores.

A young poet, Marc Alyn, compares the time of life I have reached with those big houses we see lit at night, when first one window and then another is darkened; I have come to the time of the last poem, the last novel, the last play. And now, seen at a distance, the house is nothing but a mass of silence and gloom.

Yet inside the house the same fire still burns, the heart throbs as it has always throbbed. It is crowded with presences, it is full of its own story. Nonetheless one must pretend to listen to the stories of others, although I would prefer not to think of anything except that I exist and am here. All the lamps in all the rooms are extinguished. The work is ended, but life continues, and the question posed by that life remains. I have given the answer, it is contained in my books; but now, what, really, was the answer?

As for the poets I so loved, I no longer care to know any of their verses except what my memory retains, for example, that verse of Baudelaire, that strophe of the *Contemplations,* those incorruptible shells that the sea rolls upon my sands and does not carry back again, and that short hard phrase of Rimbaud, eternally salted with the tears of a lost childhood.

Et tout homme énergique au dieu Terme est pareil.

That verse from *La Maison du berger:* as I think of it, I reconstruct it for my own use: "Every man ending is alike to the god Terminus." That is the god who stands no longer on the boundary of the garden, but between heaven and earth, on the last dune.

That ebb and flow of the sea that throbs within me, I said . . . Had I not heard these boomings, these muffled roars for many years, they would frighten me. That growling inner sea would then compel me to think of embarking on my last voyage, of weighing anchor perhaps very soon. But it does not. I am accustomed to that murmur, it is too familiar to terrify me. As a boy, I was not afraid of the sea-shell which held that moan. "Listen to the sea," they said. I no longer press anything against my ear, but that ebbing and flowing of the tide is always audible.

(3

But is it the same breaking of waves that I hear? In truth, this marine image does not correspond to what I hear within me. No, it is more like the rustling of the summer fields of bygone days. I do not hear the waves that fret the dunes, but an immense vibration of crickets and cicadas, everything that is held in this verse of Francis Jammes:

Et le brasier de l'herbe en fleur chante en dormant.

It is also that cicada that creaked alone at first, on a pine tree, until another responded, then another . . . I stood there motionless, halfway down the stone flight of steps, burning hot in the afternoon heat, a puny little fellow in a silly straw hat, bewildered in the inhuman warmth. "Don't go outdoors until four o'clock," they had warned me, "even the animals don't go out. Try to sleep." But I had disobeyed, had crossed the forbidden threshold, had entered the furnace; and suddenly I heard the cicada that I am hearing at this very moment.

Surely it is the same one. The warm breath of the earth is on my face, there is a whiff of the marshland in it. The buzzing of the summer fields of my childhood is strangely absent from the summers of my old age. But my blood remembers and recomposes it in a mysterious way.

I no longer commune with living nature. I no longer share in the panic joy. To hear that loud humming, I must find it again as in the past; in order to participate I must recall it, must resort to that "sound track" as they call it today, in which I use nothing other than the ebb and flow of the life-blood within me.

"You are creating this marvel," I tell myself, "it never really existed. The child standing motionless on the burning hot stone steps, you are inventing him at this moment. It is your old age that is creative and condemned to be so. Dispossessed of the world that is, you are obliged to regain the world that was." But to regain it is to reinvent it. That roaring in my ears imposes its rhythm on the fields of my childhood whose immense resonance was dizzying. Thus, in a train compartment, the clatter of the wheels embraces a symphony that I hear again, or scans a poem I remember, or perhaps invent.

To live is to feel in the midst of a surge of sound that death alone will stop. Silence does not exist. I wonder if this inner tumult could correspond to some page of the musical score that my long life could be said to be—if my life can be compared to a musical score. Or ought I to think that this inner resonance calls up, nay, commands, the buzzing of the fields of long ago at the siesta hour, and that this link with the past is inevitable? No, I am not so foolish as to believe such a thing. If I confound the murmurs of life in my ear with the murmur of drowsing nature unexpectedly heard by me as I stood there on the house steps in the two o'clock sunshine, it can only indicate that those minutes had greater meaning than any other for the child I was and the man I have been, since their theme singularly overwhelms me today. Yes, in those few moments I took possession of the earth, I participated in vegetal life, I advanced into a mystery that city children will forever ignore.

A poet of the city, no matter how great he is—I was thinking of Baudelaire, but he is not typical, for he substitutes canals and harbors, rivers and the sea for wild nature, in his writings—a poet who has not lived all his life in a house set among the fields will very soon betray in his works his ignorance of that secret which was revealed to me one summer afternoon more than sixty years ago. To the small portion of that secret which I have inadequately divulged in words, I owe a certain following of thoughtful and loyal readers.

It was not bourgeois pride that made me say of a certain contemporary writer, "What a pity! There's no outdoors in him!" No, it was the privileged feeling of having been granted, as I was, access to a marvel which to him is prohibited.

It is now forbidden ground to me, as well: old age has driven me from that paradise. In the neglected park to which I occasionally return, the fields have become swamps, the cicadas have fallen silent. The moaning that I now hear in the branches high above my head, is it the wind? I cannot swear to it. Perhaps the dead pines, their hearts decayed, battered by the equinoctial storms of these past sixty years, are wailing with grief, and their moans mingle with the undertow of my blood breaking against I know not what unknown reef.

However, I must not confuse the localities definitely linked with my past and those others that are linked with my present life while also belonging to the past. Even when I return to the scenes of

(5

my youth, when I walk in them as I am now doing, breathing their atmosphere, they remain somewhat unreal, they are like memories that have crystallized. This holds true of the vast grounds of Saint-Symphorien, of certain streets in Bordeaux, my school, the Grand-Lebrun. On the contrary, Malagar has a two-fold charm for me. Here the past—the long ago and recent times—meets and mingles with the present. This old manor house has shared in every moment of my life since I was born until these ultimate confines of old age. I felt this most keenly this autumn, when two photographers for a famous magazine came down to the Gironde, to Malagar, in search of my origins and to picture them for all time.

It was not so much my old face that interested them as the obscure world that shaped the individual I have become. I wondered if they had heard the phrase of Proust which I often quote because it expresses in a few irreplaceable words what I am spinning out in the present book: "The places that we have known belong now only to the world of space on which we map them for our own convenience. None of them was ever more than a thin slice, held between the contiguous impressions that composed our life at that time: remembrance of a particular form is but regret for a particular moment, and houses, roads, avenues are as fugitive, alas, as the years." *

My two photographers were trying to capture, in pictures, moments I had lived many years before they themselves were born. The strange thing is that they pursued their quarry in my absence, and perhaps some of their successful camera shots will be the best thanks to my absence. Upon arriving at Malagar in the evening, they said, "We have just come from your school. The Superior was most kind. We have prepared everything in advance, and when you accompany us there it will take up only a few minutes of your time."

My school . . . What must these sixty years have done to it? I dread the contrast between the memory I keep of it and the school I shall be obliged to see.

And here I am. I go forward, with averted eyes. The long corridor with its black and white tiles has not changed. I glimpse

---

* Marcel Proust, *Swann's Way*, translated by Scott Moncrieff, Random House, 1928

through the glass door of a study room some boyish heads bent over books, hands rumpling the hair. But the photographer leads me on: he did not need me to discover the one window at the end of the corridor which opens directly upon my unaltered past. It frames the little school, a small structure of the eighteenth century, and the picture is exactly the same as in my time. Some boys are playing in front of the steps. The Superior has turned them loose; they are astounded at this unexpected recreation period, and they are all staring up at us.

As we pass them I pause to bend over them, at the request of my camera-wizard. A final click and I prepare to escape. But the photographer has other plans. He has found the one classroom where there are still desks of my time and he insists that I sit down and lean an elbow on one of them. They are worn by the years, corroded by the tides of schoolboys—one would say that shells have remained incrusted here, like those stones that recall now vanished oceans. Among the carved initials I see a letter "M." Who knows, I may have carved it there. But so many Mauriacs have succeeded one another in this school! And here come two of them, to greet their great-uncle. I do not recognize the two charming boys, Benoît and Philippe, at first. The Superior, fighting the "black shirt" tendency, insists that the big boys wear shirts with buttoned down collars, and sober neckties. I too was once a boy of sixteen who went off down that very corridor toward that same drowsing classroom.

II

The Child's Calendar
of the Year

Those places that I said belong both to my distant past and the immediate present, to the heartbreaking fullness of time and to the burning moment I am living now, have a modest, mournful and immortal aspect that can be summed up in the manor house of Malagar. I have been reminded of this in recent days by the new regulations which have changed the dates of the summer holidays. The change has altered the most secret rhythm of my life, unchanging since my school and college days; the long vacations of the past, the interminable summer holidays, were all bound up with the changing seasons that could be perceived upon the beloved earth at Malagar and with the story of Christ that the liturgy made me resume day after day.

Life had kept for me the rhythm of childhood. An immutable order was set by the seasons and by the Catholic breviary: there was the time of work and the time of rest, the time of departure to the country and the return to the city. That part of us which does not age, that heart of a child which we keep to the end, found their landmarks in a world that has now become alien and hostile. A route was traced that we could follow with closed eyes. And now I no longer recognize it.

For some years the long vacations have begun earlier than when I was a schoolboy—but only by one week. The general outline remained the same. The beginning of the term exhaled for the children of the time the same reek of fog that it had for us; it remained linked with the falling of leaves and the migrations of birds. But from now on it will exist in my mind only.

I am not seeking here a theme with variations . . . I am wondering how to make myself be understood. We must remember that little boy who lived long ago, the boy I was, before the telephone and the cinema, before the radio, of course, and even before the automobile and electricity. I have been familiar with those salons of old ladies which were lit with oil lamps that had to have their wicks trimmed; those lamps still exist on the mantels at Malagar. In the evening the lamps were brought in and there was that circle of light on the ceiling advancing with the servant, that wise virgin, who held the lighted lamp. For us, progress still meant gaslight—that flickering butterfly of gas turned down by the night supervisor in the gloomy corridor of the boarding school, flickering down until it was nothing but a wee blue flame. The supervisor's shadow moved on the wall. He pronounced the invocations to Christ and the Holy Virgin, and we had to repeat them after him before falling asleep.

> *"Je vous donne mon coeur, mon esprit et ma vie . . .*
> *Assistez-moi dans ma dernière agonie . . ."*

Yes, we pledged our heart, our mind, our lives. But what was meant by "my last agony"? Did our schoolmasters want to convince us, thanks to this prayer, that other agonies would precede the last one? We did not try to find out what lay behind those weighty words which sank into us like heavy stones cast into a dormant pond: the pond returns to sleep, untroubled, but the water holds the stones and will keep them forever.

We children of Les Landes, those remote vast moorlands where we spent our summer holidays in that epoch before all the technical advances had brought about the bright lights and accelerated pace of the present day, were closer to the *Ancien régime* than to our own nineteenth century. The older people among whom we lived spoke and understood only the local dialect. One of our shepherds had never seen a railway and insisted on being paid in the ancient coins of the realm. And I vividly recall the guttural and almost savage songs that were sung at the weddings of the tenant-farmers. We heard at a distance the laughter and singing, along with the creaking of their carts as they approached down the rutted dirt roads, muted at first, then louder and louder.

"It's a wedding!" we exclaimed, and the cortège arrived, preceded by a fiddler. The bride kissed us all, one after the other, and one time she even kissed our private tutor, a blushing young seminarian. I wonder if he recalls it today, in his St. Sulpice cell in the rue du Regard where he is still living a saintly life.

I am calling to mind that small world of other lives to explain my attachment to that oldtime race-course through the school year, from New Year's Day to Easter, from Pentecost to Prize-Day. Thanks to the Roman liturgy the essential remains for Easter. Unfortunately it was not the liturgy that set the dates for the summer holidays. It could do nothing to prevent this change which makes them begin and end from now on a whole month earlier.

Thus, what little remained of a vanished world is becoming gradually effaced; those signs visible only to us of a life that technology had not yet mechanized can be seen no more. I recall those nights when I heard, on the wet pavements of my native town, the heavy trot of horses that the first man had broken in. The railway had become a part of the poetry in which our life was steeped. It crossed the countryside without disturbing its mystery. The railway destroyed neither the towns nor the country. On foggy nights, as I lay awake, the whistle of the train could not be distinguished from the foghorns of boats in the port, and presented to my mind a vision of vast spaces, of alien peoples, of the world's mystery which aviation has now destroyed.

Yes, the school term now begins much earlier. Yesterday, coming home from early Mass, as I walked down the road the wind had dried between showers, I was surprised to pass some close ranks of schoolboys with their book bags and their rucksacks. My heart always melts at sight of those bored little boys with their anxious early morning faces, whenever I see them pass on the great roads of France. It used to be at the end of October each year, when I was driving back to Paris, that I glimpsed them, through the windshield, fearful little migrants trudging down the fog-bound road. But this morning I realized we were barely past mid-September. Had a blind power thus decided to amputate the summer vacation of these first days of autumn, those days that had given me my first inspiration?

The thought of the summer holidays thus injured dealt me a death-blow, opened a wound that will never heal. The wind in the forest moaned a dirge, reminding me that all things come to an end.

Children are unaware of this, have no knowledge that they will die, and it is of no use to warn them. I recall that even the death of a schoolmate did not enlighten me. Death was an incredible and monstrous accident which could not happen to me, but only to others. I recall paying a visit, in the company of my family, to the dead boy's parents. He had been a friend of my brother Pierre and was the first dead child in my experience. I seem to recall that we did not enter the house but stood on the pavement of a dismal outer boulevard in Bordeaux. Perhaps my mother thought that the sight of us would hurt those pathetic people. As we stood there, looking at the closed shutters of the house, I imagined the frail corpse lying extended between his grieving parents, and pictured the scene as if it were some ghastly crèche.

The equinoctial storms, more than anything, made me believe in death. I learned about death gradually, and not through seeing my mother perpetually in mourning, nor that bedroom where my grandfather had slept his last sleep and where the bed would never more be opened, but through listening to the wind's lament in the last days of September. It struck me in those hours heavy with doom as we stood poised on the threshold of that period of time which seemed immeasurable: the school term. The school term of itself alone constituted a whole lifetime, replete with unknown risks and perils, and with unknown felicities, too.

It is in the autumn that poets are born—at least this was true in my time; perhaps it no longer applies to the language-robots who have since appeared on the scene. But in my time we responded to the poetry of autumn. I am thinking of poets such as Francis Jammes or Jules Laforgue (he would have been a hundred years old this year, had he lived). How many of us remain who can recall him? What knowledge he had of the autumn! For him it was "the coughing in the lycée dormitory of the boys who have come back to school . . ."

I began to have a premonition, when I took my last walk around the park, sniffing the air, ears strained, foot suspended—startled fawn hearing the faintest crackle of a branch. In my personal legend, the King of the Aulnes does not kill the young; he initiates them, unhurriedly, taking his time, from autumn to autumn, into a secret inscribed everywhere, certainly, but indecipherable to the child who considers himself to be immortal. Stopped in the middle of the path, eyes shut the better to feel the breeze on my face, it was a mortal philtre that I drank, unknowingly.

What kind of people are they who could be so blind as to amputate the summer holidays of that period of somber initiation? "Not all children are poets," I will be told. "Your reasons are valid only for young dreamers, a species doomed to disappear in this age of the motor-car." People who say this are mistaken. All children are poets; even the least inclined to dream among them prefer above all the seasons of the year the period of the hunting of larks in the harvested fields of rye.

The wood-pigeons were not yet passing through, but already a few of the advanced guard were arriving. To be sure, it was cruel enough to go back to school on October 3rd. But at least we had the foretaste of the season with which we were most in harmony. We returned to the city, and behind us the countryside shut on its mystery. I envied the peasants who would witness in my absence a strange magical sleep, that muted preparation for the awakening of the sleeping beauty that spring was for me.

When I should return at Easter, it would be the hour of regeneration (I did not yet know this word, but it would have pleased me had I known it, and I would have repeated "regeneration, regeneration," I would have fairly sucked the word, like a bonbon, for I did this to words I discovered). On the heath the regeneration would appear only on the banks of the stream under the greening alders; elsewhere only death would still be visible. The oaks remained full of their oldest brown leaves. The corpses of the ferns would not yet have begun to decay.

That secret the winds of autumn had whispered into the ear of the child, the zephyrs of renewal repeated it with a more cruel accent. It was like an orchestration of oblivion. Everything was being reborn, and soon there would not remain enough of last year's corpses to bury. I looked for the marks known only to me, an initial carved on a bark in August, a fossilized stone, buried in October at the foot of a pine-tree, signs of my passage at a certain hour which would not return. These landmarks could not but open my eyes to the eternal flow of things. I began to feel myself being borne along, and I clung to the branches, and I still kept myself from shouting . . . A poet was born.

Suddenly I am thinking of that time which preceded the beginning of the school term; it extended from the 15th of August to the 8th of September, from Assumption to the Nativity of the Virgin. It marked the decline of the summer holidays. That short span of time held a particular mystery, but how define it? Perhaps it was linked with forgotten wizardries. Certain herbs must be gathered between the two days of Our Lady. Where did I dream this? At any rate, there was the gathering of the nuts that would be infused in Armagnac for our provision of *eau-de-vie de noix* (the only liqueur not forbidden to us children). The nuts were beaten down from the trees during those three weeks when summer sustained its first bruises. During those days, too, we gathered the eggs that would be conserved for the winter. It is the period when the cocks take a rest and give their hens some peace.

Beginning with the 15th of August, the summer holidays had reached their zenith. On Assumption Day, the air vibrated with the chiming of bells and the buzz of cicadas. At High Mass the young girls—*les Maries*—who were not the thread-thin girls of today but were stocky and plump little ponies (we called them *"Ponettes"*), assembled in their dresses of white percale or muslin, looking like swollen flowers, blooming for a short while.

If, during my childhood, there was one single rainy August 15th, my memory has rejected it and jealously closed upon it, for I recall how we breathed in with delight those days, from the instant of waking, aware that the morning mist announced a burning hot day. The "Maries" did not lack among our cousins, and we hailed them with a crackling of fire-crackers called *crapauds*—toads; but first of all the three final strokes of the clock made us hurry a little to arrive at church for the first Mass, a low one. All the same, there would be the canticles to the glory of the Holy Virgin, and at the moment of communion, the one we loved best of all: "Lord God of hosts, Heaven and earth are full of thy glory . . ."

I would raise laughter were I to confess why certain words of these canticles of bygone days so affect me still. But oh, how swayed by poetry were we, those rather ridiculous children of the bourgeoisie! For we were surely comic in our knickerbockers fastened by elastics just above the knees and our sun-hats which made us look like mushrooms. I like this title of one of Drieu la Rochelle's works: *Reveuse bourgeoisie.* Yes, we were dreamers.

The most precious and also the most perilous privilege we youngsters had was that dream in which we lived, a dream that was perhaps the source of some surrenders and weak-heartedness. But even so, it was a privilege, and I became aware of it later on when I noted for the first time upon reading a work that did not have its origins in the dreams of a protected childhood. Not that it was necessarily of poorer quality or did not excel in many other ways; but the meanders of a subterranean stream that is dear to me remained unknown to that author. For some critics there exists a wild game whose scent will always elude them.

The birthday of the Blessed Virgin Mary, the 8th of September, was a legal holiday under the *Ancien régime,* and is so no longer. It had a hard-to-describe secularized and a rather derelict quality that pleased us. We remained devoted to Our Lady of September, like those old farmers who, my mother wistfully said, did not yoke their oxen on that day, although those same farmers never attended Mass. In lives apparently infidel, how many obscure fidelities exist!

Our Lady of September appeared between the morning mist and the evening fog. No matter how warm the days still were, autumn showed itself in the early morning hours veiled in a mist that vanished in the ten o'clock sunshine, then returned with twilight, a twilight which came a little earlier every day, for already the lamp had to be lit at suppertime. Once the meal had ended, we no longer thought of sitting outside for a while below the flight of steps, facing the stars; but we still went for a stroll in the grounds. A voice called out to us, "Put on your coats . . ." What kept us outdoors more than all the uninhabited worlds of starry space was the odor of autumn at its beginnings.

III

On Dreams,
both Waking and Sleeping

This year I was prevented from returning to Paris by road. That drive through familiar provinces that I so love, those great highways where I recognize such and such an old wall, a door concealed beneath its ivy, that ancient lodge near a gate always shut on an uninhabited property, very humble things, to be sure, but which a long familiarity illumines for me in a light as singular as if Cezanne or Van Gogh had fixed them forever. I am sure I see their equivalent through the windows of the Sud-Express train, but I do not feel the least pleasure, and no matter how fast the journey, it was too slow for me, I wanted it to end.

Moreover, the Sud-Express is nothing like the train we knew in our youth; the old-time luxury has disappeared. I remember . . . The compartments of other big luxury trains were upholstered in a commonplace beige color. Only the Sud-Express offered deep arm-chairs of dark reds and blues. I liked to smoke "Murattis ariston" and Abdullah cigarettes, pretending to be Barnaboth. I defy any young man to benefit in any way from a journey in the Sud-Express of the present time.

And so, on this last return to Paris, after All Souls' Day, I saw through the windows of a train compartment almost the same land-scape that would have been framed by the windshield of my car. But in a car I am alone. The presence of other travelers in that crowded train rendered any miracle impossible, although the Sud-Express was running, for me, in the very midst of the past. From the

minute we left Bordeaux, the rumbling under the tunnels of Lor-
mont had for me the sounds of those years before the first World
War the same significance as the three blows in the theatre: the
curtain was going up on a new year in Paris. What a wealth of
possibilities! The other travelers in that past did not disturb this
delightful anticipation: they were unlike the travelers of today;
they were also a part of the luxury, a fauna that perhaps no longer
exists. Or I may have been more capable of isolating myself, then, in
a crowd of people, than I am now. The presence of others did not
bother me. There is a time of life when we do not suffer under the
gaze of others, and there is another time when the old man would
pay a great deal to possess the ring that rendered Gyges invisible.

I return, I have returned, and the dream of Paris begins.
What else am I doing in this book but living a dream—a waking
dream, however, which in no way resembles sleep. The roaring in
my ears which I mentioned earlier, and which becomes the rustling
and buzzing of the fields in the past, that is a dream, but a premedi-
tated dream, more like a reverie, and it might persuade some people
to believe that I know nothing of the dreams born of the night, that I
have only waking dreams.

I will confess I do not like the dreams of others. When anyone begins to tell me about a dream he has had, he soon loses my
attention. I have only to know that a dream is being recounted to
stop listening or to read no further. But I have no more interest in
my own dreams which could only bore me if I remembered them. I
never repeat them to anyone, especially not to myself. Besides, how
could I, since I forget them the moment I wake up? Scarcely have I
opened my eyes than a demon or an angel effaces those images
which jostle each other and disappear, before I have been able to fix
the contours.

To tell the truth, I dream a great deal. I come to the surface
each morning from a chasm teeming with dreams, I have no doubt
of it, at least. If to die is to return to oblivion, we would be wrong to
liken death to sleep. Waking up delivers us from an illusory life, but
all the same, a life. My experience in this respect does not tally with
Proust's. He often refers to the anguish of his awakenings, especially
in unfamiliar rooms, where reality no longer coincides with his

memories. Barely emerged from the night he was unsure where he was or who he was: sleep had made of him a creature without memory, entirely thrown back to the crude sensation of existing. For me, on the contrary, to awake is to be reassured, it is to return to a friendly world which I believe I can control; it is to escape the mirages that possessed me and against which I felt powerless.

This relief felt by the Christian upon awakening lies in the fear that sleep chains the guardian which in life is Grace, the fear of sinning if only in thought or desire. In truth, this vigilance is only partly chained; an invisible hand sometimes shakes the sleeper. In the sigh of the Christian who wakes up and says, "It was only a dream," there enters the feeling of relief at not having done any wrong. But has he not done wrong? A scrupulous person does not get out of it so easily. The book he had read before falling asleep, the film he had not resisted seeing because "one simply has to see it" have played a part. He had hoped to have conjured the demons residing in them, but sleep had let them loose, all at once, across the labyrinth of dream.

In fact, there is no need to see a show or read a book to feel responsible for the images that crowd our dreams. The most troubled dreams spring from our very being. If we were to remember them, would we have the courage to look at them squarely? Merciful forgetfulness exempts us from it. The mere fact of having dreamed something proves, however, that we have been capable of such and such an act in the past, or at least would have been capable had the opportunity offered, or we desired it at certain moments of our life.

"Do penance for your hidden sins," Christ said to Pascal, "and for the secret malice of those you know." This Jansenist view of our responsibility in regard to errors of which we ourselves are unaware, and of an occult malice which eludes us, I wonder if Pascal applied it to his own dreams, to everything that the most innocent of creatures, even Blaise Pascal, is capable of doing under cover of sleep and darkness.

Forgetfulness is a great boon that has been granted us when we have barely emerged from sleep to conscious life. All the same, many people remember their dreams, and many writers recount them. Thus the law of oblivion does not always work. But no doubt, too, there are people who do not mistrust their dreams as I do, and who are curious about them, and so resort to the means I myself think of sometimes, without ever employing them—such as keeping a pencil and paper within reach to set down the dream images before they are effaced. This would be especially useful, it seems to me, in the sudden interruptions of sleep in the middle of the night: we are awake but for a short time; the wave that has cast us on the shore has subsided and we remain as if soaked with its spray; it will pick us up again and bear us off once more; we should take advantage of this brief interval of lucidity to set down on paper some landmarks that will be of use later on to guide us through the baleful forest.

I am surprised that I have never tried this. No doubt it is because I do not really want to remember, but am in league with the forgetfulness which settles for me everything having to do with dreams. But I am especially convinced that memory is concerned only with past experiences and is not adapted to the phantoms of the night. Its domain is of this world. It stores up for our torment and delight real things, creatures of flesh and blood, everything concrete through which our life began to well up and spread out like water from the ground, over stones and grasses. My memory is not fond of dreams, nor is my poetic imagination; they find no nourishment in them.

Perhaps it is a general rule of memory, this inability to mesh with dream. Yet I have often had the impression, in my dreams, not of something already experienced but of something already dreamed. I like this pithy saying of Georges Perros: "Dreams remember dreams."

It is surprising how wide the gap is between our dreams and our memory, and also that a memory is more real than a dream. We certainly feel it: to have been and to be no more, this is still *to be*, since we remember it. The head that rested on our shoulder in that brief interval of an evening sixty years ago remains there still, while as to the dreams we had at that same time, I doubt that a single one has ever risen to the surface from the abyss. Less remains of those dreams than remains of the fogs of October, the gloomy mornings of the school term beginnings, for we at least recall the smell of those fogs, while I cannot recall what woke me up with a start one night, making me cry out, and a hand was laid on my forehead: "Of what are you afraid? I'm here. Sleep."

"How old are we in our dreams?" I have wondered about this. If, as I believe, our dream-age is indeterminate, not corresponding to any precise moment of our life, we reenter, at awakening, the age we actually are. But then, why do I have that feeling of safety each morning as I return to conscious life? If to awake is to reenter our real age, then I should feel a pang of anguish at finding myself old. But quite the contrary: I disembark from my dreams, delighted to reenter my ordinary life, glad to find myself again in this closed world of my present life which is very singular, very different from the active life of young people and of the countless species of human beings who are "of a certain age," an age that is certain.

And when someone asks, "Why do you talk about it all the time?" I protest that I am not yielding to an obsession, not at all. Truly, I inhabit an island, I am sitting on a rock. What solitude old age brings us! I describe my rock, my island. The thoughts that come to me here, the inspirations that visit me here fill my time. What else can I do? An old man is always something of a Robinson Crusoe.

The misunderstanding arises from the fact that our apparent life, if we are neither infirm nor deprived of our faculties, nor slowed down, differs little from the life we led in the past and may even seem more committed, more *engagée*. We alone can survey with our inner eye the sparkling sea that extends around our rock and separates us from the world.

Not that the world has forgotten us; across that sea it sends us messages, signals, appeals, requests. It may be a preface that I am asked to write, a manuscript I must read, a photograph to sign, an inscription on a fly-leaf. Every mail brings us proofs of disinterested friendship. A writer would be very ungrateful if he remained unmoved by these testimonies of confidence and devotion. All the same, these testimonies are sent to the writer who, precisely, does not inhabit our island and who is not ourself. The writer who bears our name represents us in the outside world. We see him as he is, showered with praise and decorations—sometimes insults. The letters overflowing with admiration and affection and sometimes loathing are addressed to him, not to this creature of flesh and blood whose solitude here on his rock is intensified the more that "personage" is talked about as someone of importance in the world of men.

Some of the most celebrated men and women in the arts (Mme Bartet first of all, when I was very young) have often described to me the horror of their solitude after evenings of triumph. This is the moment when the old star confronts the mirror and wipes off a last streak of makeup from the ravaged face. As for a writer, he has the illusion of being constantly on display in his books, his plays, his journalistic pieces. For him there is the continual contrast between the personage who functions outside and the creature he knows himself to be, vulnerable, aware that nothing more can happen to him except to be, one day, struck at some turn of the road by a blow he knows will be mortal.

Remembering my youth, I recall the dark dawns. Now I want to dwell on the thought, want to experience one of them again in imagination.

It is still dark, when I wake up and listen. The quality of the silence tells me what time it is. If taxis are still on the prowl, I say to myself, theatre-goers are returning home, so obviously I had merely drowsed off and have wakened from the first sleep of the night. But sometimes, at rare intervals, I hear only one or two isolated cars. This means that some late night-owls are still about; the night must already be far advanced. The deep silence of three o'clock never fools me: no need to consult my watch, I know that I can go back to sleep until the clatter of a dustbin announces that the time has come for me to leave my bed. At about that same hour, in my boyhood, by the glimmer of an oil lamp, I hurriedly dressed in a chilly room . . .

The provincial street where we children, sleepy and ill washed, waited for the omnibus to pick us up had neither the look nor the smell of the Paris street down which I walk every day in the dark morning, a street poisoned with petrol fumes, crowded with parked cars that have no garage.

In those distant times, that rue Margaux of the town where we lived, there was, in the left wing of a solemn old house, a Jesuit chapel called the Margaux chapel (it has been secularized for many years). Waiting at the bus stop, my brothers and I, we could see some poor women flitting through the fog toward that Chapel. We called the poor souls "old bigots." And now I'm the one who goes through the dark dawn to Mass, where the housewives deposit beside their prayer-stool not only their market basket and their bottle of milk, but the burden of the day that is beginning and of the night that is ending, and also the crushing weight of poverty, sickness, and perhaps also betrayal and desertion. And I approach the altar of God, of the God who gladdened my youth.

So here I am, among those men and women who come because they no longer have anything except this comfort which remains, that is to say, everything. I recall what someone once said regarding old age: "Saintly old age rejoins saintly childhood, but not in the pathological sense; it does not mean sinking into second childhood when one discovers, thanks to the inner eye, that the passions of life have not stifled the child in us, the child of whom it is written that his guardian angel sees the face of the Father."

In the ill lit street I make my way with difficulty among the refuse bins that encumber the pavement, and wedge my way between the parked cars. The bakery and the bistro that face each other cast a glaring light on the pavement, but very soon afterwards the darkness becomes so dense that I sometimes stumble against a dustbin. I push open a door and am now sheltered from the street, from time, from mankind. I have embarked on a vessel where One unseen by me is seated at the stern. The vessel pulls away from shore, yet without moving. I shut my eyes. The souls of all those people massacred in these endlessly sinister days may have followed me as far as the door, but they did not enter with me. I will find them again as I leave. The souls that surround me are the same ones that I saw more than sixty years ago, shrouded in fog, on their way toward the Margaux chapel—old people . . . However, it sometimes happens that a boy or girl is kneeling not far from me, but almost everyone is a specimen of faded and finished humanity, and I mingle my own shadow among all those motionless shadows on the brink of eternity.

Not that youth has lost in my eyes any part of its charm, God knows, for not a day passes that I don't shut my eyes or shake my head to banish a face, not a day that I do not uproot from my heart that fresh herb which indefinitely springs anew. But, meditating on my own youth, I reflect that it prevented me from rejoining Him from whom, however, I was not utterly separated. It is merely that He who was necessary to me at every turn of my life has now become the sole necessity. In my youth I was unable to attain to Him, as I can from now on. When I was young, even if no particular passion obsessed me, that hum and buzz of youth were enough to daze me and turn my mind away from God. But now He is revealed to me by an inner silence and emptiness, and I possess Him to the degree that I am dispossessed of all else.

Even so, it was the same presence the fifteen year old boy foreboded as he stood waiting, at half past six in the morning, on the corner of the rue Margaux and the rue de Cheverus for the bus to arrive. The clatter of the wheels on the cobblestones, the crack of the whip announced it from a distance. My bag swollen with books was less heavy than my heart. "My heart was heavy," we say. My mother did not know that it was a renewed grief for me every morning, the thought of being separated from her during the whole day.

"But, in truth, I have wept too much, the dawns are harrowing . . ." Had I known this line of Arthur Rimbaud at that time, it would have become my motto, and the bourgeois little boy whose hooded coat ill protected him from the cold as he stood on that damp pavement in Bordeaux would have felt he was the little brother of the vagabond poet who, thirty years earlier, had climbed the rue Monsieur-le-Prince at dawn, on his way up to a furnished room.

Oh, dark mornings, how I should have loved you! Cities change from one epoch to another, not only in aspect but in atmosphere and odor. In winter, however, shortly before daylight, I find again, fleetingly, the smell of wet asphalt that I inhaled as I waited for the bus. The street lamps of my ill lit neighborhood glimmer above that same hurrying humanity, fearful of being late, at the hour of greatest gloom, between sleep and labor. None of that has changed, and the schoolchildren also hurry, their faces unsmiling and already with that frown between the eyebrows and perhaps with hearts as heavy as mine was, heavier than their book-bags weighed down with unlearned lessons, unfinished homework.

On Dreams, both Waking and Sleeping

How well I remember those early risings in the dark and chilly bedroom, my feet and hands swollen with chilblains, and how well I recall the hostile schoolmasters, the jeers of the class when I stood paralyzed at the blackboard, and the classmate who, at recreation, took advantage of his strength, using it on me! But none of all that misery altered a secret joy: the waiting for the sixth hour, the return home in a winter mist that already smelled of Christmas. That happiness flooded my life as a schoolboy, gloomy as it was, and sufficed to dispel the anguish.

It is always Christmas in my mind and heart, at the season of "the dark dawns." In winter, every Mass is linked for me with the miracle of the Nativity. Everything comes to mind at once: the fireplace in my mother's bedroom where the fire was never allowed to go out, became on Christmas eve a route which linked the dark room to the stars that were no longer indifferent or blind because someone would come down that road to us! We knew nothing of Father Christmas; we were sure the visitor would not be the Lord . . .

But now I know that it is He. The old Simeon clasped Him to his breast. Delivered from the cradle, resuscitated from that first Passion, the cradle, the Child, in the arms of the old man, would for the first time hear the beating of a human heart; He would be loved, not only by His mother, but by the old man who trembles with joy because his eyes have seen the light of the nations, the glory of Israel, and because he will be able to sink peacefully into his last sleep.

That Canticle of Simeon, that *"Nunc Dimittis,"* is the prayer of old age to holy infancy,* the Canticle of Gertrude, the old abbesse, at the end of her long life: "O my Love, the love of the evening of my life, rejoice me with the sight of Thee at the hour of my departure. O Jesus-of-the-evening, make me sleep in Thee a tranquil sleep."

Yes, it is always Christmas when I look back on those dark mornings, those of today as well as of days gone by. Walking slowly along the wet pavement, I draw my cloak over the Holy Child given me, as perhaps St. Simeon did. But it is not only in my arms that I hold Him; henceforth He is within me. I have become that cradle

---

* Luke 2:29–32

which stood in a stable open to all the winds, where other animals less innocent than the ox and the ass have left their droppings. I warm my Infant God within me.

My mother's bedroom . . . The lamp sketched on the ceiling the aureole which for me forever haloes the heads of saintly women as they sleep. The great bell of the Saint-André cathedral booms, and the sound of that bell ringing out above the rooftops of Bordeaux mingles in my memory with the verses of old St. Simeon's Canticle which I have been meditating. The past is found again, not as in the book of Proust, because of the taste of a madeleine cake and the scent of a cup of linden-tea, but because the birth of God has introduced me into an eternal present.

We will have been nonetheless that young man and this old man, we will nonetheless have lived that guilty life, that troubled destiny; but above the stagnant waters Grace brings forth, like those statues of gods rescued from ancient shipwrecks, a small dark and pensive face, kept intact in the deep slime, that very face the candles of the crèche in my grandmother's bedroom bathed in their gentle and flickering light.

I V

The Books and People
of our Childhood

I interrupt myself at this point to give myself a scolding.
Having sworn to guard against my bent to indulge in pious reflections, for I detest having to listen to devout Catholics when they
yield to the same inclination and pose as saints, there I was, doing
exactly that . . . As if I were unaware that the most mediocre
Christian, if he is gifted as a writer, can orchestrate the most ordinary words of piety and give them an exaggerated resonance!

I will not erase what I have written, but shall try as much as
possible not to succumb again. How far will that "possible" go? Shall
I be able to resist my natural penchant? My first volume of memoirs
crystallized around the readings of a lifetime. I believed I could go
on writing until my death about that immense reserve of ingurgi-
tated literature that I have assimilated during more than sixty years;
I had thought this literature would never cease to nourish a singular
work that is, properly speaking, neither a diary nor memoirs. But I
was wrong. That armature composed of everything I had read has
given way, little by little, under the pressure of a flood I tried to
dam up and contain. What is happening?

Are the books going to be shut, one by one? And this "never
more" that I hear emanating from things and people, am I also to
hear it come from that imaginary world where, since my childhood,
I have taken refuge from the real world? And all I demanded of the
real world was merely to be given enough leisure to pursue, shel-

tered from living men, an interminable confrontation with fictional characters, or to seek, in the works of essayists and memorialists, paths that intersect with mine. Is all this really finished? Is all this a dead letter?

The lack of any desire to add to my collection of records is serious enough, but worse still is the fact that I ask almost nothing of the records I possess, as if the vague roaring of the tide which is bearing me along drowned out all music for me from now on. No, don't tell me "It's because at your age, the source of all love has dried up, and with it, music . . ." It is not that simple. The inner source continues to well up and even to gush forth more strongly, but love, instead of spreading out as formerly among all creation, now measures itself against the immeasurable. But it is true that even the most inspired and purest of musicians, even Bach or Mozart, no longer embody those states of mind that some people of my age know, where silence is no longer silence, where the ebb and flow of the tide I spoke of (life, withdrawing) mingles at night with the heart-throb we hear when we press our cheek against the pillow.

But after all, if I am so easily resigned to cast music practically out of my life, while my growing indifference to reading troubles and disturbs me, it is because music, unlike literature, never was of utmost importance to me. I entered the realm of music whenever I liked, but remained an alien, a barbarian. Music was for me what the ocean is to summer voyagers: neither sailors nor fishermen, they do not depend upon the sea for a living, they ask nothing of it except some moments of happiness on the margin of their real life.

On the other hand, what would remain of my past life without books, my own and those others that have strewn my path since infancy? What is left of my life after subtracting printed matter? What, after all, is that part of me which is not dependent upon literary criticism? At my death, what will be that poor little thing struggling in the fisherman's net?

Certainly I go on writing just as I go on breathing. I believe that as long as my heart beats and my brain is irrigated with life-blood, the usual words—we always employ the same ones and would be amazed to note their limited number—the words will come to the tip of my pen before I have summoned them, faithful servants who know my habits and manias, and the balance, the number, the euphony, all the secret code I use, all the formulas to which I have disciplined them.

The page is written before I realize it. I was never so in command of my pen as now, when it performs its task almost alone. A professional writer such as I am no longer needs to think about his craft, no longer needs to be constantly supervising it, and has gone to join the novelist in I know not what back-stage region of my life. There remains this old man who no longer tries to fashion or imagine anything, but merely reflects upon himself and listens to himself as if, in this constantly thickening twilight, the word of the enigma would suddenly tremble at the tip of his pen and write itself down on the white page. This explains why I so easily do without what was formerly the indispensable intermediary between myself and myself: reading.

My first volume of musings, which I called *Mémoires intérieurs,* was an effort to account for myself by examining the literature I have most loved. I now tend to put aside those dimmed mirrors where my actual face is no longer reflected. That face of a twenty year old boy that I once was and who is still reflected there has become alien to me. It was for that young man and not for me that literature was an enchanted palace with a maze of corridors through which he wandered from room to room. In every one of them was a sleeping princess. Today, for me, all the princesses are dead; I have lost the power to waken them.

Those who see me living would shrug if they heard me, and would say, "As if you weren't always surrounded with books and still are! As if you have ever stopped reading!" Indeed, I apparently continue to read and write. But I no longer participate in what is recounted, no longer confront myself with those tragic masks that have become nothing but masks. The people I know who are mad about the theatre, well, they seem to me literally mad. Actors are all lunatics.

All the princesses are dead. Did I say that? Yes, and I wonder if Phèdre herself has not returned to oblivion; if not, then why does each actress who tries to give her life seem grotesque to me? All the corpses of all the last acts, and which resuscitate at every presentation or reading, there they are, stretched out around me, for good and all.

To confound my inner life with the books I have read, as I did in the first volume of these musings, was to use a subterfuge. Yet what else could I do? I see now: my inner life has ceased to be a story I can tell. At my age, the inner life no longer has movement. It moved for many years and to the very confines of old age, but is now calm and motionless. Nothing happens any more. On the high and narrow plateau where I have settled, no more "suspense" can be expected. All that remains is the long winding road of my past existence that I have finished with and can look back upon; there it is beneath my eyes, the whole journey from childhood, and I can discover nothing new, nothing that is not already known to me and which has already nourished my dreams.

The first books I ever read put a more indelible stamp on me than did any later masterpiece. Children's books are absorbed thirstily by an earth open to whatever falls upon it from heaven, from the best to the worst. Not that as a child we were not already critical. I was a born critic; as far back as I can remember I was a critic. When I call to mind that good nun who so frightened me when I was five, I see her exactly as I saw her then, and those schoolmasters I had at the age of seven and eight, I still regard them with the same critical eyes, they still seem formidable to me. After more than sixty years the picture I have kept of them needs no retouching. But the child, never mistaken in his judgment of people, makes mistakes in his judgment of books, or at least (for the child from the child's point of view is right) he does not expect of books what he expects later on, while already demanding of people what he will always demand, no matter how long he lives. He demands that they be good, that they be just, that they be intelligent and pure.

At the age of ten I thought *Les Camisards,* by a certain Alexandre de Lamothe, was a masterpiece, and thought so for reasons that no longer exist. But I already saw why my schoolmaster was unjust to me, a little boy with a shorn head and no pretensions to beauty, while he gave exceedingly good marks to the curly headed little boys. "Men do not need to be handsome," was a golden rule in our family, and it greatly consoled me, for I was brought up to think of myself as ugly. This exercised our humility. But at school I learned, all by myself at the age of seven, that children need to be pretty.

Returning to the books I read in my childhood: I have often tried to dip into them again and find the enchantment of bygone days. In vain. Nothing was left of it. The schoolboy who devoured books had created the enchantment. With his vanishing, there remained a text too insignificant to have kept the least sparkle.

That sparkle appears only in the books where, no matter how slightly, literary concern is displayed; for example, Hector Malot's *Sans Famille*. I have not seen the film that was made of it, and would not see it for anything in the world, but I am again dipping into this enchanting story which I first read sixty years ago and picked up again many times later on, for it is a book that has never wearied me. The remark made by the venerable Royer-Collins to Alfred de Vigny, "Monsieur, I don't read any more, I *reread*," is the remark of a child more than of an old man. Children, at least children of my kind, were fond of the books they already knew; they skipped the gloomy passages when rereading them, and lingered over the pleasant incidents. I reenter *Sans Famille* today as if entering a house where I have lived for a long time: I open the shutters and move from room to room, from chapter to chapter, my eyes half shut; I recognize those rooms by their smell. The enchantment revives, weakened by the years, but fortified by this miracle of experiencing it again.

I am ready to believe that I myself contribute to the crystallization that takes place around that juvenile tale. But am I right to believe it? There is reason for self-examination if what remains of poetic feeling within us is no longer stirred to life except by trifling things, while the authentic poets of today exercise no power over us. Yes, perhaps I should eat humble-pie.

Hector Malot would perhaps have been very distressed had he known he would survive only thanks to a book for children. What a cemetery is romantic literature! Or rather, what a common grave! The grant of a grave in perpetuity which each author calls his *oeuvre*, with the fictional characters' names clearly incised on the marble, is soon obliterated with the brambles of oblivion. Those characters destined to resuscitate have already done so and that small number of the elect scarcely increases from century to century.

But Rémi, the hero of *Sans Famille*, is among those privileged ones. I have only to read the first phrase of the first chapter: "I was a foundling . . ." and that violin bow strikes a chord that opens for me a singular symphony. I recall exactly the shabby volume I carried into the farthest end of the grounds and these words penciled on the flyleaf—about which my brothers laughed uproariously —"This book is beautiful because it made me cry."

The book no longer makes me cry, but it still melts my heart. However, my interest in it is not solely linked with this fondness for going back to sources that is so characteristic of old age. The same interest was stirred in me last year when I rediscovered *Jacquou le Croquant,* by Eugène Le Roy. If the characters at times are described in the most artless and banal way, the great roads of old France are so vividly depicted that an entire landscape of the past comes alive, snow buries the roads, wolves howling at night frighten the vagabonds, and we feel intensely the bitter insecurity of the poor, their unspeakable suffering in that time . . . But was it worse than today? Perhaps not, but it had another tinge, was of another kind, at any rate.

I am not sure whether I read *Sans Famille* before or after *Le Tour de France par deux Enfants,* which was too technical for my taste. But it was a good way of introducing the avid boy reader to the secrets of his native land. The route those children took followed the Garonne river to Langon, then crossed Les Landes on our road, the one that goes through the Bazadais region, quite near that part of the family property where I was reading the book *Sans Famille* . . .

Although these books were published before I was born, I recognized every turn of the roads; they were the same as the roads rutted by wagons in the flooded heath, down which the wheels of our carriole jolted. In my youth the matrons of the small nearby market-town recalled having heard the howling of wolves, and over toward Chalais, in the Charente, wolves were still to be found. How I loved those great roads! I envied the muleteers who drove down them all night long, lying in their carts, faces upturned to the stars, arriving in Bordeaux whenever their mules liked . . .

We are told that the motor-car has revived the old routes, but in fact they were revived only to be destroyed by the car. Its cancerous multiplication has eaten away the tree-lined borders. The old elms were the first to go. Now they are felling the plane-trees, and the roads of France which used to have a familiar and irreplaceable aspect will soon all look alike and become one long and monotonous speedway.

At least, this is true of the highroads. When, driving toward Malagar, I turn in the direction of Chevanceaux shortly after leaving Barbezieux, I suddenly enter the real country roads of bygone times; they are still so deserted that they seem spellbound. The abandoned roads I am thinking of still greet the wandering troupe of *Sans Famille:* Rémi the foundling, old Vitalis, Joli Coeur, the monkey, and Zerbino and Dolce and Capi. The lost child at the village cross-roads sings for me alone, in his dialect, and plays his harp whose gilt has been washed away by the rains:

Fenesta vascia et patrona crudele
Quanta sospire m'aje fatto jettare.

But he too looks for that boat called *Le Cygne,* and the great English lady (I guessed from the first pages that she was Rémi's mother!) who voyages with her invalid son on the canals of France. As it happens, the Midi canal flows into the Garonne river at Castets, almost at the very gates of Malagar. And if, as Pascal says, "rivers are roads that move," he might have added that canals are roads that sleep. The canals sleep, and horses were the motive power of the swan-boat on which Mme Milligan voyaged with her son. Oh, the busy life of the rivers and canals before the coming of the railroad!

"How beautiful it must be on the screen," I said to someone who was telling me about the film made from *Sans Famille,* "especially that story of the cow Rémi bought as a surprise for Mère Barberin." But the film had forgotten that cow. How lucky I was, not to have seen that film! For it would have destroyed that unique world, known to me alone, where my childhood becomes a part of the France which existed before I was born and before the motorcar; a world still wrapped in solitude, the subtle perfume of solitude and silence.

A better world? No, of course not. But the people of a certain race breathed more easily in it, I believe. The harp of the child Rémi will no more attract people to the village square, because they have the radio and even television in their homes. Mme Milligan would no longer have the delightful idea of taking her invalid son for a voyage on the canals and rivers of France. Nothing today resembles that bygone world, except for people of my age who carry it within them. Yet we sometimes find it again and identify it at a turn of a road in the country, muddy and trampled by the droves of cattle, or we recall it when we hear the owl in the autumn night or a dog baying at the moon and reminding us of the time when the wolves still prowled.

I was the creator of my joy—which was a physical joy, in part, due to the attitude I assumed for reading, propped on my elbows, chin on my cupped hands, fingers stopping my ears, so that nothing in the outside world could distract me from my delectation. Strangely enough, this joy reached its peak just at a time when I was most unhappy. In October my mother sometimes lingered on in the country for settling accounts with the tenant-farmers, and for the wood-pigeon shoot, while we children returned to school in town. Then, according to my ideas at that period, I became, for those two weeks or so, the most miserable creature in the world: a boarding-school pupil. Everything was horrible in that life when I was separated from my mother and home, everything was unendurable, except the very long study hour in the evening and before dinner on Sundays and Wednesdays when, the day pupils having left the school, we had the right to read whatever we pleased. Then, comfortably settled at my desk, in the gentle warmth of the stove, some sweets within reach, I devoured the book I had taken from the glassed bookcase at the far end of the study room.

The books were very different from the ones I had at home. Alexandre de Lamothe figured prominently among the authors. There were his *Les Camisards, Les Faucheurs de la mort, Pia la Sanpietrina* . . . Am I the only one alive who recalls those marvelous titles? I had no idea whether they were more worthy of admiration than the complete works of Mme de Ségur or Zénaïde Fleuriot which comprised, along with Jules Verne, the essentials of my personal library (not counting the complete files of the *Saint-Nicolas* magazine from 1887 to 1894). The books at the boarding school were of a different and therefore pleasing "vintage" with an unfamiliar taste. Then, too, the most interesting ones were always in such demand that I could not read them whenever I liked or keep them for long. Once procured, the book was a precarious possession, and one had literally to gobble it up. The stove roared. We attended to it ourselves. The nougat we had bought at the fair during the afternoon recreation was a bit too sweet. There was still a long time ahead of us before the quick meal and the silent climbing of the stairs toward the dormitory.

But these juvenile books by no means help us to visualize the little faces bent over them or to recall those children's lives. Must I then, as in my first *Mémoires intérieurs*, return to the great books I have loved? The only thing that forbids this is the risk of imitating myself. An idea crosses my mind: without interrupting my musings on the books I read as a boy and throughout my life, why not amplify by looking for that reflected glimpse of myself, not merely in the works of genius but in the individuals who are no more, recalling them as I saw them in my youth, retouching as little as possible the image I have retained of them?

The men and women I am thinking of are dead and forgotten; I will offend no one by dragging them out of the oblivion that covers them. For individuals do disappear, and many are the families, too, that become extinguished. The Christian names flourish eternally, but how many family names that were once borne by a numerous progeny end up by becoming effaced in village cemeteries on tombstones marking graves that no one visits any more!

The flood of memory that flowed through my reading, why not make it overflow to those neglected graves? I will pull up the weeds of oblivion, I will unseal the tombstones blackened by so many winter rains.

What subsists of those people long dead? No more than subsists of the dead of today. For in those past times, a corpse was dressed as if for an afternoon of paying calls. The old ladies spent eternity wearing their fine bonnets that tied under the chin. I recall that some of my relatives reopened the coffin of one of my great-aunts because they had forgotten to put her prayer book in her hands. All that world of the dead will be resurrected on Judgment Day wearing their Sunday best, and the ladies will fancy they have just returned from High Mass.

I would only have to waken them, take them as they appeared to me . . . If I bring myself to do this, I must take care not to look them in the face but to raise my eyes, for they are adult people and I am a little boy, the youngest of five children, the puniest, the one to whom nobody pays any least attention. I shall observe them from the ground up, keeping my ears wide open; their picturesque language is close to mine, the books they read in the past are the same as mine, their universe is my universe. I was a witness they did not mistrust. How many times did they interrupt themselves with, "Be careful, the child is listening . . ." "Why no, he doesn't understand." Well, he listened, and he understood.

Yes, that is a path I could follow, without neglecting the path staked out with the books I read in the past. And always there were the changing seasons, the summer holidays, the return to town, the departures in sunlight and the returns in the evening mist; they will imprint their immutable order on this resurrected world one last time, before it sinks with me into an eternity from which there is no return.

V

Maiden Ladies in my life

Even so, the idea of resuscitating that bygone little world came to me while reading a book—neither a child's book nor what is called a great book. It was a book of souvenirs by an author who was then still alive, though aged, a poet who was never a part of the circle of writers who inspired me, but who greatly resembled the beloved writers of my childhood: *Les Notes intimes,* by Marie Noël, that Christian soul dear to the Abbé Mugnier and the Abbé Bremond. Her book has become my constant companion these days.

Marie Noël was a person made to measure for Father Henri Bremond, who has caught her portrait exactly in his scholarly book, *L'Histoire du Sentiment religieux en France.* Or rather, he has given us the portraits of all the Marie Noëls of the French provinces during the past three centuries. The provinces are well stocked with them and their breed is not near dying out. Wherever there is an altar, a tabernacle, you will find some of these saintly spinsters. Their inspiration, if they are poets, comes to them from God, but not an imprecise and vague God. They commune with Him every morning. They do not need to tell us this; their daily presence at the early Mass reveals it, and it is there on the communion table that the love of their life is consummated.

Why did I stay away from Marie Noël until this late day? I suppose it is because we who loved poetry in our youth become all the more attached to the poets who embody it for us, and our hearts shut out all others. From a certain age on, we admit no newcomers.

Paul Valéry, toward the end of World War I, must have been the last poet who somehow forced his way into my heart and mind. Even Apollinaire will always remain outside, if on the threshold. Since Valéry, no new voice has mingled with the familiar chorus of my poets: Baudelaire, Verlaine, Rimbaud, Claudel, Francis Jammes, Anna de Noailles. As for Marie Noël, I was stupidly prejudiced. I imagined her as another Eugénie de Guérin, but without her brother Maurice. And if I read Eugénie, it is because I am fond of her brother.*

I have, indeed, no least reason to speak flippantly of the "old maids" of our provincial bourgeoisie. But I was prejudiced against a poetry that sprang from those lives I knew all too well, having observed them at close range as a child. I can advance with eyes shut into the life of Marie Noël, and without stumbling into anything, so familiar to me is the locality. I recognize in it even the fragrances. I have seen all too many frail shoulders crushed under the weight of that cross: the burden of each day's thankless toil, the apparently sterile labor of a maid-of-all-work.

Marie Noël's *Notes intimes* reveals what I sensed in other maiden ladies of our small towns or country districts, women who almost always grow old in the service of their families, of an old and demanding mother, or wasting themselves on the children of others.

The saying goes that they have "lived a great love"—a love experienced intermittently but undiminishing and undying, quite different from so many human passions, and this love will have remained the great if not the unique affair of their lives. And human love must also have prowled the desert roads where Marie Noël advances in the wind and the rain.

Her poetic work sprang from that passion which she discloses in her *Notes intimes*. Indeed, we glimpse the reasons which alienated her from marriage. We recall how coquetry was frowned on, how full of despair was a girl at the awkward age, how many of our little provincials were resigned to ugliness and celibacy, although they were in fact pretty and made for love. We could write a life of Marie Noël (but it's already been done by Raymond Escholier) without other references than those she gives us in her "intimate notes." All the essential data of a sacrificed existence are there. Nonetheless, at the very beginning it is clear she had a vocation for the perfect life, a call to the mystic marriage. That young daughter

---

* Maurice de Guérin (1810–1839), author of a prose poem, *Le Centaure*. His sister Eugénie (1805–1848) published some of his letters, and a *Journal*.

of an Auxerre family was one of the elect. Her union with God was, however, to be consummated without the succor of any religious rule, and outside convent walls. Marie Noël, without the coif and veil of a nun, followed a certain path and perhaps went farther than she herself knew.

She starts out with the most ordinary trait: the proud Mammon of wealth exercised no power over her. She is held captive (as perhaps I also was) by a paltry but demanding patrimony, an inheritance she was expected in her turn to hand down. On that inheritance the happiness of her life must depend. "Because my family had landed property," she writes, "a few decrepit buildings, and because the family was comprised of old people, methodical, set in their habits, and domineering; and because they had misfortunes and afflictions, I have lost the essential of my life, its grandeur, and find myself without a home to call my own, without relatives and without riches. But I have recovered life's grandeur, have found again its freedom in my total disinterest in possessions."

Decrepit buildings, but not a home of her own. She would just barely have a room of her own. Who was it condemned her to such a life? She was not a weak person, that girl. Her destiny was not that of persons unable to fight and win. In fact, she submitted to a law: an infinite demand weighed upon her destiny.

In how many Christian lives must there have been signed, from infancy, a secret pact! The story of Thérèse Martin, the little saint of Lisieux, is in fact a most banal one. She wrote bad poetry and became a great saint. Marie Noël, a true poet, was in truth sanctified not more humbly or obscurely than was St. Theresa in her Carmelite convent. But for the one, it was in her poetry that she became known to the world, and for the other, it was in her piety. The two young girls were caught in the same trap. Listen to Marie Noël again: "I was twelve years old that day in May, when I went through the cathedral to go to my class. The church was empty, I was alone in the church where one must not talk or touch anything or walk fast. Suddenly I dropped my school-bag on the floor and ran to press my forehead passionately against the altar, demanding of Jesus the wedding ring . . ."

What followed was not what the world calls the consolations of religion. But religion is not consoling; it is crushing. It is a great love, as it should be. Marie Noël's experience is that of everyone bent on the great adventure which is not offered solely to a few of the elect. For we are all loved, and of each one of us everything is demanded: "Be ye therefore perfect, even as your Father which is in heaven is perfect."*

Thérèse Martin and Marie Noël were to know all there is to know of the worst of trials: moments when their faith seemed to be deserting them, hours when their faith was maintained only with an almost superhuman effort of their will. "The terrible hour when God is not true and when I continue to love Him, all the same," wrote Marie Noël. In the *Journal* of St. Theresa many notes have the same ring.

Marie Noël allowed herself to be destroyed by her family. She spent her Sundays in meetings of a Church Guild, while privately dreaming of Salzburg, a free and happy life full of enchantments. Marie's self-examination helps us to realize why the humility of the saints is neither feigned nor affected. They see themselves in the light of Christ. "I perform good deeds," writes Marie Noël, "I am not good, I am broken in. I accept sweetly what goes against the grain, but I am not sweet; I am assassinated. At heart I revolt, overthrow, strike, break everything ruthlessly. But every morning Christ entices me to my destruction. And I have become exactly like one dead from having drunk with Him the wine of one condemned to die."

What renders her unlike the little Theresa is her warm heart, her constant need to renounce all human tenderness. Some of her poems tell us more about this than do the *Notes intimes*. These notes do not describe the outcome of her endeavors, but rather her moments of passing gloom, one of them longer and more agonizing than the others.

Marie Noël had this human consolation: her poetry. Quite early in life she knew she reached other hearts, knew that her verses were read, loved, understood. She experienced simultaneously the love of God and a modest worldly fame. In the evening of her life she was able to declare that she had never hurt or troubled anyone.

She was among those poets, almost non-existent today, who avoid the self-opinionated avant-garde, who are loved by those who love poetry quite apart from set codes and literary fashions. Even

---

* Matt. 5:48

her readers who share neither her faith nor her hope, benefit by the love which bore her up, sustained her, and inspired the songs with which she lulls the sufferings of others as she lulled her own. For we are all alike, in spite of our different lives; and all the hearts of a certain breed share the same story.

I have known many Marie Noëls. How many of those "old maids" of my childhood escaped the ridicule with which those two words are charged! For me, they never aroused anything but images of purity and tenderness. Looking back, it seems to me that the maiden ladies of my childhood always came in pairs. People said, "the Ducasse spinsters," "the Desbarrot spinsters"—and one of them was always more brilliant, the other more retiring. In no way did they have a part in the universal corruption. They were creatures preserved in houses and gardens that seemed to have been secreted by themselves, houses and gardens in their own image, where as a child I delighted to spend a few days when we were invited to visit the spinsters, especially the pair who lived in a remote part of Les Landes called Jouanhaut.

We played no games there. Nothing happened in that world whose frontiers were odoriferous kitchens, a company drawing-room redolent of beeswax, mysterious attics where a litter of puppies had been born, a dark stable where gleamed in the dim shadows an animal's big glistening eye. What gave value to these common and ordinary things had to do with something I realize only today: the road went no farther than the spinsters' home. Thus I associated their house with the idea of a refuge beyond which nothing lay. That region, of all imaginable expanses of land the least picturesque, the poorest, the dullest, was a refuge! I recall a field of millet, with here and there a half dead chestnut tree standing as a witness to a very ancient epoch. And all around the property stretched the vast heath, without any other road than those traced by wagons, leading toward abandoned sheepfolds or small farms.

The road led no farther than to the maiden ladies' house. What obscure satisfaction did I find there? I felt inexpressibly safe in that remote part of the world, as safe as one could be on earth. To be sure, I already knew this protection to be illusory, knew that in this country without a road death could find its way as elsewhere. The father of the ladies had come home to kill himself in a room of that old house, after his financial ruin, and I knew it. I also knew

(39

that an assassin, by name Daguerre, had been hunted in the nearby woods and that one of our dogs had found him, half starved to death.

That countryside was a refuge only according to a certain notion of mine. But nothing could change the fact that during those long empty days at the edge of the millet field I was completely imbued with a deep feeling of security that I have never found again since then, as if I had returned to curl up in my mother's lap, safe once more in the most secure refuge in that wretched land which my ancestors had abandoned with their flocks and their wild language of which certain words were unintelligible only a few leagues away.

According to my childish notion, the maiden ladies lived there in perfect bliss, in an eternal summer vacation. I did not imagine, although I had read so many good books, that the ladies could have had a heart and that the heart could have had a history. The maiden lady who was deaf had once been pretty, people said. But what did beauty matter! That enchanted little world at the end of a road which stopped there gave me the feeling of something that would never change. All else would change, but this at least was unalterable. The very idea that one day nothing would remain of this pathetic paradise was something I was utterly incapable of imagining, so fixed in an eternal being seemed those shabby farms, that wild-rabbit warren of low, thick-trunked oak trees; yes, all this seemed fixed forever, as if fossilized in a time eternal.

Oh, had I known as a child that one day fire would consume the trees and the stones, effacing everything, leaving nothing of that beloved universe! And yet I must have looked at all these things intently, as if I wanted to be sure never to forget them, for they have remained as if engraved in my memory. We carry within us the work of an admirable artist we will never know. The canvases of the great masters are only pale reflections of my inner universe which sometimes surges up through a word, a phrase.

Had those maiden ladies still been in this world at the time of the conflagration, they would perhaps have burned like fragile vine shoots, in their "company drawing-room." But they had slept their last sleep long before the disaster. They must have had the death of wise virgins, with their lamp always lit and provided with oil, they who spent their entire lives in the service of others, attending the sick, adorning the brides, washing the dead.

Asleep for so many years, those maiden ladies are, however, less dead than the ancient land they embodied for me; they are so alive that I sometimes confound them with other maiden ladies who have existed, but whose stories I know only through history books or even through the imagination of novelists. When we pronounce, one after the other, the names of Eugénie de Guérin and Eugénie Grandet, the less true of the two ladies is not the one Balzac created; and I have difficulty in distinguishing them from the maiden ladies I have known, on whose narrow bosoms I can still see the glimmer of a golden cross.

In England and France they have inspired an entire novelistic literature, as they have been the source of intense fraternal loves: for example, the Brontë sisters, the Guérins, and also the Pascals, the Chateaubriands, the Renans, the Rimbauds . . .

The maiden ladies live on eternally, while no one will ever again see that wasted visage of the heath in that part of Les Landes now being remembered, for it has been wiped out forever.

But I am well aware that the earth is that schoolchild's slate where each generation traces signs that the following generation will erase. Even so, there still exist gardens where those old people would feel at home were they to return, and houses where they could walk through the rooms with their eyes shut; this is what still attaches me to certain parts of this world. But everything has been said by Proust on the subject I am expressing here, and that last sentence of *Du Côté de chez Swann* achieves, it seems to me, a miracle of style, since in it the most complex work of French fiction is compressed into a few words: ". . . remembrance of a particular form is but the regret for a particular moment; and houses, roads, avenues are as fugitive, alas, as the years." * That phrase has a heartbreaking truth which renders futile everything I have written here about maiden ladies, it is a phrase which opens like a door onto the unique world of true poetry: puddles left by rains of yore glitter in ancient furrows. It is the rutted road that went no farther than the house of the maiden ladies, and which I journeyed along tonight among the phantoms of charred trees, on my way to a loved land that exists no more.

---

* Marcel Proust, *Swann's Way*, translated by Scott Moncrieff, Random House, 1928

VI

Meditation on Death

One of the sources of my poetic imagination was undeniably that home of the maiden ladies in the sequestered hamlet of Jouanhaut, seven kilometers distant from Saint-Symphorien, in the most remote part of the great fire-blasted heath. True, there were many others. When my brothers and I, accompanied by our young priestly tutor, went in search of the sources of the Jure river, we never found them, because the water seeped out everywhere through the inaccessible marshes. So it is with all poetry, including my own.

I must have secretly thought of writing as soon as I came into conscious life, at about the age of seven, when I began to consider reading as a door opening upon an enchanted world. Books did not free me from the real world, in which everything delighted me, even its tribulations, but they filtered reality, preserving only what the imagination and the heart desired.

That I could ever belong to that quasi-divine race of writers and poets never even crossed my mind. Although I had already written some poems at about the age of ten, the ambition to see them printed and published one day would have seemed to me the most foolish of follies. Yet I do recall having imagined (but as a happiness barely conceivable) that later on I would be able to contribute to such periodicals as *La Veillée des chaumières, Saint-Nicolas,* or *Petit Français illustré.*

There was slowly forming in me, during those years of childhood and adolescence, substratum of impressions from which would spring the source that Barrès was the first to discern, and I believe it was a piece of good fortune that I had no thought of utilizing it until rather late in life. I am glad that no least preoccupation with taking up the writer's calling, with writing seriously, came prematurely to disturb the process obscurely going on within me. Poetry sufficed. I can appreciate today the charm of the hours I spent on those poor verses that eventually became the volume entitled *Les Mains jointes,* for poetry does not use up the layers of impressions being laid down within us during our first years. Instead, it maintains them, springs from them like a fountainhead but falls back again, enriching us, one might say, with the alluvial deposits of our discoveries and our reading. Prose, on the contrary, the writing of fiction, exhausts our reserves; I tremble when I see so many young writers put into their first narrative everything that fills their life which has scarcely begun.

In my time, we made our début with a volume of verse, the first poems dating from our schooldays; almost always they were mere imitations. Nothing was subtracted from our own resources. The secret treasure remained in us intact, each day augmented, the raw material that was to furnish my fictional works, the human drama that I bore within me and, to use the words of Thomas à Kempis, was comprised of "the divers movings of nature and of Grace." But I was none the less attentive to the happenings around me, to the conflicts, more intense in families, which were microcosms I observed with the naked eye, or rather, since I observed nothing consciously, I absorbed, and would find again one day, according to a process which, with Proust, became a method and to which all works of fiction more or less owe their existence.

All works of fiction? No, not all. For many of them do not have as their source the childhood of the author. I was visited the other day by a twenty-four year old poet who has published nothing as yet, although he obviously has the novel-writer's gift. Well, he remains as if crucified by a cruel and perhaps atrocious childhood, unable to cure his wounds by writing. Malraux once pointed out the difference between us: he detested the early years of his life, his work closely embraces the present. His work is that of a man who confronts his condition and the drama of his epoch at the very moment of writing; his work is lacking in nostalgia, is without a personal past, without childhood. While, on the contrary, my works have remained as if glued there. I have never quite emerged from my childhood. For me, writing fiction means to win back and recreate that en-

(43

chanted world, which was really quite commonplace and un-eventful, reduced to elementals, when compared with all that life showered me with in later years.

The enchantment lay in a state of grace natural to childhood, which made me breathe and move in a transfigured universe, trans-figured like Van Gogh's kitchen chair and brogans. The corridor of a third floor in my grandmother's house in Bordeaux, where at twi-light my mother went to and fro reciting her rosary, or the evening prayer with her in her dimly lit bedroom—and all the rest. For there was not one minute of my days and nights that was outside this symphony, a pastoral symphony, mainly, because the months spent in town were only a period of waiting for those months we would live in the midst of fields and trees.

Nor have I ever left that countryside, nor have my works, and doubtless this is what I am praised for by those who have liked my writing—and condemned for by many others who consider it a failing. All the same, I have never dragged in trees as a useful stage-prop. That land and that sky are forever within me and are therefore in the books I have written. I should say, rather, those lands and those skies, since nothing could be less like the moorlands of Saint-Symphorien and the Jouanhaut of the "maiden ladies" which served as background for my childhood and early youth, than these horn-beam walks of Malagar and the terrace of Malagar, to which we almost never came before my eighteenth year.

Then why do I not in these musings concentrate on the story of my beginnings? Why should I not make live again all those human beings that I carry within myself, every feature clearly delineated, as did Gide in his *Si le Grain ne meurt?* I attempted it once, and the attempt was called *Commencements d'une vie,* a few pages only. What, then, made the pen drop from my hand?

When I question myself I see, first of all, that my most distant memories have escaped me. We believe we remember our third year, but in fact we merely remember remembering. I was barely three when my paternal grandmother died, and I have always imag-ined that I can recall seeing her in the vestibule of the Langon house, sitting beside a small table that is still at Malagar, in my bedroom. I see myself stealing a chocolate from her, and see her laughingly threaten me with her cane. Is it an image I find directly in me? No, I recompose it according to a faded old photograph.

The darkness covering my third and fourth years are pierced by a few brief flashes of consciousness, and two or three scenes stand out. For instance, there was that mountebank who called out to us on the road, as my brothers and I fled, and I see myself toiling up the big field of Malagar, streaming with tears, still believing I am being pursued. And again, I see us walking in a procession through the vineyard to that uninhabited house, carrying bouquets to "Grisette," intoning an incantation, a tune I can still hum. Grisette was a she-ass and we were really practicing idolatry, the very idolatry the first Christians were accused of practicing, for according to certain pagans, those early Christians worshipped a she-ass.

But all this, if I were to insert it here, would only repeat what I have already written in the little book I referred to. From the same period dates a stay at Bagnères-de-Bigorre. The villa we lived in was that of the Comtesse de Pénautier, a name that charmed me. Among all the lovely daughters of the countess, there was one who ate balls of polenta "to put on weight," and this caused my mother to attribute Turkish origins to the great lady, for the Turks, she said, liked fat women. Many years later I learned from my mother that our hostess had usurped both the name and the title, that she was only the lady-friend of the Comte de Pénautier and that we had thus spent three weeks under the roof of a kept woman.

From the age of five on, I escape from discontinuity. From then on, my memories crystallize around the school. The nursery school in the rue du Mirail, kept by the nun, Sister Adrienne, would be the first chapter of my story, were I to tell it. But that chapter would still be steeped in legend, would be set in a world I am not completely sure of remembering. My book, *Commencements d'une vie,* has fixed the few luminous points that remain in my mind. But even as to the scenes in which I figure, I am not quite sure I remember them. I cannot separate what I have seen from what I have been told. For example, that last time my paternal grandfather came from Langon to visit us in Bordeaux only one or two days before his death. In my mind's eye I see him sitting in my mother's bedroom. He is looking at the photograph made of my father by Nadar, and several others, among which he points out his own and sighs, "What a cemetery! Everyone dead but me . . ."

I was five years old and I was there. But do I remember? That scene serves as prologue to the story of my grandfather's death which I heard constantly repeated during my childhood. It was a terrible and marvelous story, for my irreligious grandfather had not set foot in a church in many years. The lady, an old friend of his with whom he played whist every night, implored him to go to church with her. He consented, and it was on the way home, in front of the Merlet spinsters' house, that he fell dead. His dying words were, "Faith saves us." From then on, in the great empty Langon house, death was present, death crouched in the depths of that bedroom which was always shut, and I recall half opening the door to frighten myself.

A hecatomb surrounds my beginnings! The shadow of death enveloped me. When my mother opened her armoire, I saw my father's hat, enormous and black, that she had kept. That father had gone suddenly, before I came to conscious life, and I knew nothing of him. There again a legend was created around the last moments of that unbeliever: the crucifix that his hand tried to bring up to his lips—according to my mother. But my grandfather insinuated that "it was to scratch his nose!"

I have transfigured a gloomy childhood, have made what was banal sound enchanting. I have that ability. Is it a strength or a weakness? A weakness, I believe; meditating upon my life I have been thrown back to a period when others took charge of everything for me, lived and died in my stead.

The people and events of my childhood could be treated historically, detached from the ray of light I shed on them. Many illustrious writers before me have done so in their memoirs. When the writer is Chateaubriand, the story of the man merges with the story of France, but when the writer is François Mauriac . . .

How vain of me to arouse from their sleep and give importance to those people from whom I issued. They could go on sleeping peacefully had not one of their descendants been incapable of doing anything else but write . . . No, I will not waken them.

From the age of five, there are no more dim intervals in my life, the entire road is illuminated. It goes from the nursery school, with its smell of the chlorine used to disinfect the toilets, with its voices of man and the clapper of Sister Adrienne which she used to secure attention. Sometimes a little girl crossed our courtyard and we boys yelled like savages: "Hi, little girl! Hi, little girl!" Or else we would stand around a pathetic little boy with wet breeches and a puddle forming at his feet, and would be yelling: "Oh, you little stinker!" Without knowing why, all this horrified me. I can imagine the unhappiness of infant animals by recalling that period when I was the little puppy separated from his mother, the pathetic little boy whose ink-stained fingers were rubbed fiercely with pumice-stone by Sister Marie-Laurette.

The consciousness of unhappiness dates from my seventh year, when I entered the school kept by the Marist fathers, in the rue du Mirail. Although I spent my time reading, I was always at the bottom of the class! Resenting this injustice I once spit on my weekly report, rubbing out that unjust mark with my handkerchief, rubbed so hard that I made a hole in the paper. I was not spared from hearing that such acts lead one straight to prison.

In fact, were I to tell the story of my childhood I could depict it in a lugubrious or radiant light. Everything depends on the stage-lighting. But I do not intend to tell that story; I recount it only to myself, and this, indefinitely. I can even make a song of it when I recall the tune of one of those canticles which would horrify people today, but I am sure those songs initiated me very early into the knowledge of "the God of peace and love."

I revive my childhood only for myself. I do not invite the whole universe to attend that resurrection of a small world of bygone times, whose secrets I never learned, moreover. What was the hidden life of those men and women? Whom did they love, desire, hate? It is for myself that I try to unravel what comes from them, what thoughts and dreams of mine sprang from one of those hearts that throbbed long before mine and of which there now remains not even a pinch of dust, in that burial vault to the left against the wall, at the far end of the Langon cemetery.

I shall not resuscitate them in these memoirs, but I do so every morning when I take Holy Communion. Just now, in this pure and cold morning, as I sit beside the fire of vine-shoots I have lit, my thoughts remain in the church of Langon, from which I returned a while ago. The church of Verdelais, nearer to Malagar, has a black Holy Virgin, much venerated. I reflect that when I pray beneath the familiar vaulted roof of the Langon church for those who have preceded me into their last peaceful sleep, I do not need to evoke my forebears one by one, but need only to let my thoughts dwell for a moment on all those ancestors who have prayed in that church or the church of Verdelais. They all came, at some time in their life, at least when children, to kneel at those altars; and even the remains of those who were not pious were brought back for burial. That grand-father, that father, that uncle, all of them opposed reason to dogma, but they too were rescued and laid to rest in the old eternal bark.

I think of them every morning, as I gaze at the three portraits—Copernicus, Galileo, and Descartes—still hanging in my bedroom, placed there by my infidel progenitors. These pictures correspond to the religious pictures in my mother's room. And I, too, love Descartes, who continues in my mind to argue with Pascal.

The infidel grandfather and father, those stubborn unbelievers, were nonetheless choirboys in the Verdelais church, when they were pupils of the Toulenne school which no longer exists. And they have returned. They have been rescued, as I said, and brought back in the old net full of starfish and algae. Everything shall be saved which seemed to be lost. I do not invent this, for it is written, "with God all things are possible."*

Perhaps one single faithful soul in every family suffices to draw after him all the others who are not faithful. That little boy who takes communion beside me, frail as he is, carries the salvation of an entire breed. From generation to generation, that torrent of love carves its course through baleful heritages. It is not merely the faithful wife who sanctifies the infidel husband. We never pray without all our kin praying with us. Redemption does not merely concern us as among the rescued, but as rescuers. Every staunch Christian in a state of grace is a redeemer. Whoever understands this is delivered from despair.

"Where did you get these ideas?" you will ask me. "They do not derive from the logical reasoning esteemed by your father and grandfather, but from the faith your mother professed." I would be hard put to reply.

To believe, to have faith—what does this signify? It seems to me that the act of faith is more deliberately made than is generally thought. Faith, or religious virtue, demands an effort and constitutes a victory when achieved. It is a refusal to refuse. What devout Chris-

---

* Matt. 19:26

tian has not at some time in his life been close to yielding to the lure of negation, and what agnostic, what atheist, has not yielded in some form or other to the lure of the Father which is in heaven, or has not felt a desire for purity and pardon? Who among them has not had to struggle against the nostalgia of the lost childhood? Thus the human tide will flow to the last day toward the Father and ebb from Him. It is eternal love that regulates that tide.

Yes, I see some shoulders being raised in a shrug, I hear quite clearly someone calling me an old fool who does not know what kind of world he is living in and who does not realize he is only a fleck of mold on the surface of an insignificant planet in this cosmos comprising quintillions of solar systems . . . Yes, but that ocean of galaxies is conceived in the mind of a single human being. Thinking man is truly at the center of the cosmos, since he thinks and measures that cosmos, immeasurable though it be. It seems to me that redemption is far from being ludicrous in relation to the cosmos; whereas the cosmos, devoid of thought, blind and deaf, has little weight when compared with the brain of a single human being, and still less weight when compared with one single heart capable of loving and suffering.

"You are always quoting your Pascal," I will be told. Yes, and how can I help it? The music of the spheres in the infinite spaces would not exist except it be heard by a single man. It is absent if man is absent. Such is the color of my thoughts on this icy cold morning when I have been living in close communion with my dead.

How strange that generations should have trembled at the thought of the dead. O ghosts, why do you never return? The first night of these Easter holidays I heard some regular tap-tapping at one of the corridor windows. And I recalled hearing in my childhood that this house is supposedly haunted. Some insect or bird was perhaps caught between the shutters and the glass. I preferred to imagine that a sign was being given me—of course, without believing it! Never has anything come to me from that shore I am approaching. Nothing has ever happened in my life that I could interpret as an appeal.

However, to my way of thinking, the silence of the dead is by no means to be confused with their absence. They are mute, but so long as I am here they too will be here, and not merely as images

among a host of others. Our Christian faith makes us live in familiarity with the dead, not because we adhere to a doctrine that con-
fers survival on them, but because the Christian world is founded on
reversibility and because the communion with the dead maintains
incessant exchanges, a dialogue that is endless—yes, a dialogue that
will go on forever.

But why waken the dead? To revive them in these memoirs
would be to condemn them to die a second death with me. But at
this point I question myself: if I renounce my power of resurrection,
then of what does this book I am writing consist? And this brings
me again to ask myself, what is the substance of my life that is
coming to an end? What can an old man tell, a man to whom
absolutely nothing more ever happens? But here is the marvel: it is
after that "nothing more" that he penetrates the unique reality.

In the past, I could not remain a second without doing something. To stay as I now do in my bedroom and not even take up a
book—I doubt that such a thing ever happened to me formerly; or if
such a thing happened it was because I was devoured by some care,
was obsessed with some grief, some scruple . . . Nowadays I often sit
motionless, attentive to a life that is only life, without anything to
distract or hurt or flatter me. No longer do I merely "spend time." I
am submerged in time, I am overflowing with a muted life that has
never seemed so inexhaustible as at this hour of decline when, according to nature, I know it is about to run dry.

The truth is that no thought holds me as I imagine thoughts
hold the sages. On one of these recent evenings I happened to open
Alain's selected essays. And I thought of André Maurois and that
entire group of intellectuals who still regard Alain as their master.
"There," I said to myself, "this is what helps them to live and this is
what will help them to die. This is their nourishment and it fortifies
them." But as for me, I mumble a few phrases and spit them out, as
if instead of bread I had been offered, as it is written in the Gospels,
a serpent or a stone.

Is there no common source for the self-communion of the
pious and the meditation of the sage? On the contrary, I believe in a
unique source—but I also believe (which is folly in the eyes of
agnostics) that they do not perceive anything but the reflections of a
light whose primary source they ignore or deny; whereas the most

mediocre Christian, no matter how small his fund of love, has the presentiment of that fire which has burned the faces of the saints; for they almost all have been licked by the flames. Their feet and hands have sometimes been pierced by a burning dart and their heart has sometimes been transfixed, like that of St. Francis of Assisi in the Florentine painting my friends in Reims gave me. That picture dominates my study in Malagar, and every day the Saint blesses me with his raised hands stained with blood.

No, it is not a voice the Christian hears when he remains motionless, eyelids lowered. Of what does his happiness consist? Claudel ridiculed those who talk of the "consolations of religion." He knew what it costs the saints to be saintly. "It is not a laughing matter that I've loved you." This remark, addressed to Angèle de Foligno, has been heard by countless saints! Even so, Claudel would have humbly agreed that for the common run of pious men such as he—and still more such as I—religion is in fact, and in the most human meaning of the word, a consolation and help. No, that says too little; it is a pleasure, and not because of the promises of eternity with which it showers us, for it is one thing to believe it and another to let it nourish one's meditation. "*Saintes douceurs du ciel, adorables idées*"—to quote Corneille's *Polyeucte* once more, you do not preoccupy my thoughts, although I do not doubt you. But it is here and now, upon return from early Mass in that deserted church, that I feel too happy to think of doing anything else but "attend the fire," as my mother also did, upon returning from Mass. All the dead, I can still see them here, on the low slipper-chair, attracted to the flames and the ashes. I can see them, elbows propped on knees, handling the same tongs I am using today, arranging the glowing coals according to the method they bequeathed to me.

Were they as happy as I am? For we are now concerned with happiness, and not with consolation. In fact, I am not consoled for anything, either for my secret griefs or the public abominations or my private life or the criminal history of humanity.

Consoled for nothing, but happy, and happy even over what would formerly have afflicted and troubled me, as for instance, over having been almost the only one attending Mass this morning. Formerly such solitude overwhelmed me: to think that light came to this world and was revealed only to a small number, and to think that of this small number the majority should have rejected and despised it, what a stumbling block that was for my faith, at times! But today, now that the great witnesses have left us, they who fortified us by their example and their word, men such as Claudel or Bernanos, the small number of those who believe what I believe does not trouble me. These weekday Masses are like a fire I come to sit by; it burns only for me, in the midst of a few servants, and I feel like Simon-Peter in the High Priest's courtyard on the night of his denial of Christ. Except that I, at least, would not have denied Him. And I kneel on the same prie-Dieu which, padded with straw, used to hurt my thin schoolboy knees.

Am I afraid of death? Yes, I am afraid. Has this fear marked my whole life? Shall I reply with a yes or a no? "The thought of death deceives us, for it makes us forget to live." That was the theme topic set in 1904 for the Bordeaux Bachelor of Arts degree candidates. Astutely I took a negative view. "You will get either a 0 or 20," one of my professors warned me. Well, he was wrong. I did not get the lowest or the highest mark: I received 18, thanks to Pascal, for I followed his reasoning step by step, being already steeped in this thought. I would like to reread that old paper of mine. But where, O Holy Virgin, are the papers of yesteryear? Were they burned at the time? If so, they were reduced to ashes a little too soon, for they prefigured everything we would later write.

Were I to write on the same subject today, my paper would have another sound, I believe, for there is a verity that I ignored then and know today: the thought of death does not deceive us because, in fact, we never actually think of death, even when we try to. Perhaps we will die without ever having confronted, even for a second, the idea of that final moment.

Although death cannot be looked at squarely, I do not believe that the impossibility has to do with the horror we have and which must be surmounted. Death eludes our comprehension only because in the absolute sense it cannot be grasped. It exists somewhere between the dying breath and life eternal—or oblivion. It is always against one of those three terms that our thought collides, without being able to apprehend anything beyond them. The passage from one to the other, from time to what is no-time—who has ever been able to conceive it?

As for me, I am so constituted that I shrink from imagining anything outside human time and space. My faith and hope avoid any representation of such a thing. My faith and hope are of time, and they accompany me to the last conscious hour of this duration which will have been my life. Without the Incarnation, I doubt that the idea of God would have been conceivable to me. By the Incarnation, the idea takes on flesh and blood, therefore time and space, and so forth. I am no longer concerned with what begins beyond life. It is up to the Lord to keep His word; it is for Him to be at the rendezvous He gave to all mankind and in particular to each of those who have loved Him.

But how prepare for death if we cannot focus our thought on it? Today I know what I did not know in 1904 when taking that arts examination: this preparation for death is indistinguishable from detachment. To prepare for death is to untie one by one all the bonds that hold us, it is to break as many moorings as possible, so that if the wind suddenly rises, it will bear us away without our putting up any resistance. It is a detachment which takes place within us and does not visibly betray itself, does not affect our exterior life. And as to the individuals with whom we cease to be in contact, we need have no compunction on that score: they are the ones who left us, they took upon themselves all the pain of the uprooting. One day we will perceive that no one is attached to us except those who are so attached that they are as if a part of us. Never will a stranger enter our life again, never more will there be someone within our restricted circle who has come from the outside world.

Nothing is demanded of us except to consent to it. But is it not hard to think of relinquishing certain things? By comparison with the marvelous possessions of others, my booty of a lifetime seems paltry indeed. When I itemize today the objects that have always provided the setting for my life, they remind me of what as a child I called my treasure: it was a box with a sliding lid; in it I kept my agates, the brilliant stones collected in the Pyrenees. The things scattered about on the console tables in my home are worth scarcely more than the agates of my childhood.

As for my house and garden, I do not feel the need to detach myself from them: their existence is already quite spiritual, and I will take them with me.

But there is a knot that the writer cannot undo, even with a stroke of a sword: his bond with everything he has written, his *oeuvre*, or rather, that image of himself in his writing which he has given to his epoch, or believes he has given—that foolish hope of survival in the memory of men, that idea of an ineffaceable vestige, of a footprint miraculously captured and held, stamped forever in the dust of the road.

Even if my reason leads me to believe that my work will perish, nothing can erase the fact that ever since I became a writer I have seen my life in the light of the books and plays I have written. I still sometimes think, "That was the year of Barrès' article praising me," or "That was the year when *Genitrix* was published," or "the year of *Asmodée*," or "the year of the Nobel Prize . . ." Each of us has his secret hegira, an era that is exclusively ours, with its triumphs and disasters. In others this illusion seems incredible or comic, until reasoning by analogy compels us to recognize that we deserve the same ridicule. We believed we were the center of the world, and in effect we were, but it was of a world we invented for ourselves and it will vanish like our dreams, of which it was for a moment the condensation—a drifting mist that will perhaps persist for a little while, between heaven and earth, when we are no longer here.

My mind could never encompass death. Yet the dead I call mine have never left me. At every moment of my life I seem to have been hemmed in by their constantly increasing throng. But those from whom I was separated in my youth remain the closest, despite this uninterrupted increase. If my memory should fail, if one day I should lose control and succumb to forgetfulness, the dead who left me first would also be the last to be erased from my memory. Not a day or night passes, I believe, without their faces looming up, if only for the space of a sigh. Sometimes it is one, sometimes another, some of them at long intervals. And it is not always the faces of those we most loved that are called to mind; it is as though the fact of having been a part of the life of a child or youth was enough to give them the right of priority. Some of them whom I regarded with indifference at the time have become dear to me, upon reflection, if I may put it that way. I offer them now what they expected of me when they were still on earth—an affection that I did not dream of giving.

But there is a vast difference between remembering the dead and concentrating one's thought on death, one's own death, as if merely to evoke the non-visible, the non-existing transported us into a stifling atmosphere. The man who thinks about death is like a deep-sea fish drawn up on the beach. Oh, how great the urge to plunge again into time and space and to frisk about there!

Strange that age in no way alters this feeling, strange that in old age the contemplating of death is no easier than it was at the dawn of life. All those men and women who every day fall beside us, this rapid shrinking of the human group with whom we have traveled, is of less help than one would think.

Morever, death struck as sudden blows around me when I was scarcely more than a child. My mother never laid mourning aside. What an expenditure there was on crêpe veils in these oldtime families! The young, far from being spared by death, were the most frequent targets. Pulmonary consumption—that disease which no longer sows terror—menaced us all. Altitude as a cure was not dreamed of then. An entire young generation agonized and died facing the sea, under pine trees that have never cured anyone. The war of 1914 devoured only those among us who had not been "taken off by the lungs," as the strange saying went. It is true that one of the servants of death, pleurisy, performed her work badly, touched us only slightly, and not only did not kill us but rendered us unfit to carry arms and thus unfit to be killed.

I have seen at close range whole families wiped out by tuberculosis. Those hecatombs should have paralyzed me with terror and distracted me from any other thought. Especially since the literature I loved was filled with dying young poets. Thus I followed Maurice de Guérin step by step in his calvary, from the rue du Cherche-Midi in Paris to Cayla where he breathed his last.

Yes, I should have succumbed to terror. But the knowledge I had of the death of others never became transformed into sensation: I did not feel mortal, although I knew I was. Do I know it better today, when it no longer concerns a fear of something which can possibly be warded off? There is now no room for doubt: I am approaching that moment. Every step I take brings me nearer. I am like a man who sets out at dawn toward the sea he has never beheld. He is separated from it only by one last sand dune. He hears the roar quite near, he tastes on his lips a terrible salt. And yet he remains incapable of imagining what he will see tomorrow or tonight or at any minute.

What's this? you will say, astounded that I, a Christian who believes in life everlasting, have not accommodated myself to death any better than pagans did. I confess. It is one thing to believe in immortality and another to visualize it.

Even a very intense faith and an unflagging hope do not make the contemplation of death any easier. To fix the mind upon the separation that awaits us, on that parting from everything that holds us, animate and inanimate, turns out to be less a meditation on death than on the results it brings about. Death is not an uprooting but an engulfment, hence as unthinkable as being. We jib at the idea, we brace ourselves at the door of the slaughter-house, incapable of even imagining the horror and terror that sinister darkness can hold.

But it would be yielding to the pleasure of the macabre to deny the strength we find in our faith, in the promise that was given us and in which we will believe to the end. The prayer of Saint Gertrude in her old age to "the love of the evening of her life," that tender supplication, "Let me fall asleep in You and sink into a tranquil sleep," recalls the lulling to sleep of an infant in arms who has only to shut its eyes. But above all, no matter how indifferent a Christian believer may have been, he shall have known during his lifetime that commencement of love for God demanded of us so that our faults may be forgiven; if prayer, the sacramental life at certain hours, shall have given him a foretaste of what the contemplation of the saints can be, all this will suffice to let him glimpse the fact that the night in which he will be engulfed is an illumination and that the unremitting solitude of death opens upon a peace and joy of which at times he has been granted a fleeting taste here on earth. That love to which he will go has already been possessed.

He will have been united here on earth to what he is about to contemplate: heaven is the substance of our hopes.

The Incarnation is the mystery of a God who traveled the entire road toward us, and who was not only one of us during His mortal life but has remained with us, and that is not all: He dwells within us. This being so, how could we aspire to find Him elsewhere if we possess Him here on earth? I recall the canticle of my First Communion: "Heaven has visited the earth . . ." Yes, and it has done more than visit the earth, it has merged in it without annihilating itself, so that to die will be not only for us to leave the earth but also to leave the heaven that we have possessed in the flesh, even in the humiliation of sin and its tears.

What I am saying here must seem strange to you, and you wonder if other Christians feel the same. You are afraid of discovering the sign of an adoration not always turned toward the infinite Being, but toward that carnal part of yourself which from infancy has yearned for a "pure love."

The more you examine yourself on this point the more you will find in yourself this singular distortion: your inner eye cannot direct its gaze forward and can only be focused on the past. You are always that child who preferred the worst place in the carriole, on the back seat; the child who turned his back upon the horizon, the trotting of the clumsy old horse, and saw only the muddy or dusty road unrolling between the carriage wheels, like the tape-measure the servant Octavie paid out from its box.

Thus, what your eyes continue to devour is not what lies ahead of you; your death day which will perhaps be night or twilight or dawn, toward which you are traveling, no longer in a carriage but drawn onward by the constantly accrued weight of the years; instead, you are constantly contemplating the past, which you are leaving farther and farther behind.

At this point the comparison with the road unrolling between the carriole wheels is no longer apt. For what you see resembles more the ocean deeps in which nothing is lost. Above the abyss of the years, the water remains clear and conceals nothing of what it covers over: certainly all the faces, gardens, roads, but also the seasons and the hours, the smell of the playground at four o'clock in

(57

June or when the winter froze it, and that chocolate bar tinfoil picked up in the dark and deserted courtyard streaked with the beams of light from the classroom—and that school-mate who was not your friend, to whom you never spoke, and yet whose name rises to your lips like a bubble to the surface of quiet water.

Yes, that quiet water holds more than these very paltry things of a child's life, and this is what I am trying to say. All the stars tremble in the depths of that quiet water, the stars of the holy nights when we sang in chorus, "God of peace and love, glory of glories," but also, and more beautiful than the stars, the flames of every First Communion Mass which reminds you of yours, when you discovered that happiness, too, has need of tears. O childhood full of God!

It is God, alone, that you have carried away with you from that childhood. All the rest had to be abandoned, but not that presence indissolubly a part of your very being, so much a part that you doubt if it can possibly be found again after death. Rather, you almost cannot believe that He whom you will contemplate in the hereafter can resemble that Friend you have on earth; your eyes do not see Him, your hands do not touch Him, yet He walked beside you in the dark mornings on the damp pavement of the rue de Mirail where your school was, and He is still, today and forever, keeping step with you. Between that past and the present was a man's life, similar to all men's lives, woven of ambitions and desires. The river of the childhood paradise had disappeared underground, but now it has gushed up anew in the wilderness of your last days.

Every time one of my fellow-writers passes away and I am asked to say something about him, my idea of death clashes either mildly or rudely with that of the agnostics and atheists. The same war of religion has been pursued from one deathbed to another, from that of Jacques Rivière to that of Gide.

One summer morning in a sunny hotel bedroom I heard the radio broadcast: "Colette has died." Again it was in a hotel room that the name of Roger Martin du Gard suddenly asserted itself as if already carved on the stone that would cover him. The departing friend does not go without laying his hand on our shoulder. There enters into our grief that fear which kept us awake when as a child we heard a furtive step in the stairway. The prison of the men born before 1900 is emptying, and we who write are no longer numerous, while waiting to stand up in our turn when our name is called.

Martin du Gard . . . We rarely met but we somehow felt close to each other, were fraternal adversaries. He did not excuse me for anything in a certain category; the war of religion was waged between us, I believe without hatred on his part, certainly without hatred on my part. That obstacle kept us apart. We were kept apart by the different answer we gave to the question posed at the very beginning of our lives, a question that disturbs writers of our kind, born in a Christian land of bourgeois and conservative stock: Are you going to conform, or rebel? *Jean Barois* was the first response of the young Martin du Gard, and *Les Thibault*, in volume after volume, comprised the definitive brief drawn up by that offspring of a fine old family against his bourgeois class, scrupulously conscientious, concise, expressed in a faultless diction which well served his cause. In this respect we were drawn to each other; on a social and political plane we reacted similarly. But, I repeat, our war was a war of religion.

That war found complete expression in the public debate which began between us at the death of André Gide. I had commented on Gide's last words. "Are you suffering?" Professor Delay had asked him. And Gide—I am quoting from memory—replied, "Yes, the struggle between reason and unreason continues."

I would not insist that the remark could have a metaphysical connotation; I merely advance the idea as a hypothesis. Jean Delay, to whom it was said, had no doubt on this score. And thereupon, Martin du Gard flew into a passion.

This incident throws light on the argument over Gide that raged among those connected with the first *N.R.F.* magazine, at a time when Grace had touched so many souls: Jammes, Dupouey, Ghéon, Rivière, Copeau, Du Bos, among others. In relation to Gide, his tutor and friend, Roger Martin du Gard stood firmly on the side of "what is reasonable." The two men had been bound to each other by their differences; like a bindweed, like a convolvulis, Gide held that solid and upright spirit, faithful to naturalist techniques, attentive and strict reader of his master's manuscripts. But that master, in revenge, had helped him to become what was called, in that circle, a "free spirit." Chronology is very important, and I have no way of

(59

verifying the date of their first encounter. Whether it was before the composition of *Jean Barois* I do not know, but it is a fact that the Gidean attitude toward life could determine the attitude of Martin du Gard—again, I am unsure to what extent. It does not entirely have to do with immoralism: Gide proved this for himself in a large portion of his life which was highly exemplary. The intellectual honesty of Martin du Gard was so well known among us that his name could not be pronounced without evoking that strictness which was his personal stamp. But what fire burned beneath it! How suspect, in his eyes, was a Christian, especially when confronted with the mystery of death! I recall those sinister disputes over the dying Jacques Rivière. It was as if the Catholics were always on the alert, thinking of nothing so much as to add another name to their list of converts. And it is quite true that we do not cease thinking of our death and the death of those we love, but not in a spirit of conquest. Because, for the believer, this passage from life to death determines everything, for it is the moment of final Grace.

I doubt that any sentiment is so disinterested. True, as we think of a dying friend we think of ourselves as well. It is a trial for our faith, at those times. We, in our solitude, are being caught in a beam of light that others do not see. The light came into this world and mankind rejected it, but perhaps it was because they did not see it. Why did they not see it? Oh! I, who am accused of Jansenism, I would not have been among those who so easily resign themselves to be among the small number of the elect.

I believe with all my heart that for each one of us, as I said, the death agony is the moment of final Grace. That is why I attach such importance to the last words of Gide. The eternal possession of God's love or its eternal absence—this, for the believer, is the alternative confronting everyone in the throes of death.

One of Martin du Gard's close friends wrote to me, protesting this point: "That the sole moment which counts for the soul's salvation is that of the final death-rattle, that in the eyes of God a man is not what he tried to be during his whole life but only what he is as he lies dying, his mind wandering, afraid, this sort of thing makes me resolutely withdraw into the ranks of honest thinkers. There is no Catholic belief as shocking as this to a free-thinker, I assure you . . ." What a misunderstanding! For who would ever believe that a gesture and a formula pronounced over an unconscious dying man or one with a wandering mind could ever save a soul? As for the dying who yield to fear, to a sordid calculation ("Since all's up with me anyway, it won't hurt to try . . ."), I have no idea how they will be judged, but it is true that from the human viewpoint they are rather contemptible. One of the blackest lines Balzac ever wrote was that cry of the dying Mme Marneffe: "And now I *must* receive the Holy Sacrament!"

This has nothing to do with the illuminating Grace I spoke of, that Grace which descends when the dying man perceives at a glance his paltry life strewn with acts as they really were, and at the same time perceives the love he had not recognized and which calls to him for the last time. But all I could write to my protesting correspondent on this subject is contained in a passage of St. Luke which he had read many times, I imagine: Christ's words to the good malefactor. Everything is said in those words. The horror of what he has been overwhelms the dying man, but he does not despair. He sees himself, knows himself, and at the same time sees and knows that a single word of veritable love suffices to save a criminal life. In this connection there is no more touching story than that in Saint Theresa's "History of a Soul," the story of how this Carmelite nun, then unknown, interceded for the assassin Pranzini, condemned to die, and who, almost to the very end, cursed and rejected all religious thought. Then, at the last second, on the scaffold, he kissed the cross with a reverence that left the witnesses amazed at this unimaginable reversal. "Verily I say unto thee, to day shalt thou be with me in paradise."*

Recently I ran across these lines of André Malraux, taken, I believe, from *La Tentation de l'Occident:* "True, there is a higher faith, that which proposes all the village crosses, and even those crosses that dominate our dead. It is love, and appeasement is in it. I shall never accept that love, that appeasement." This conclusion which so ruthlessly contradicts the premises and falls like a cleaver, like the blade of the guillotine, casts a light on the singular peril, in a Christian perspective, that is run by the dying man whose last hour will be watched, and who knows that in a single minute the significance of his whole life may be altered.

---

* Luke 23:39–43

"In Martin du Gard," his friend wrote in that letter to me, "there is no least thought of an after-life. But I guarantee that if there are chosen men, he is among the elect."

Certainly I also believe and hope this. But let us forget that dead person who was dear to us, let us put aside any personality. For here we are touching the very crux of the misunderstanding. Between a life that is honest and upright according to the world's judgment and a life lived according to Christian requirements there is a vast difference. Not that the strictly natural virtues and qualities of the upright man are without value for the soul's salvation. But the precept, "Be ye therefore perfect even as your Father which is in heaven is perfect" * has an absolute significance. The discernment we have between good and evil, the significance and the effect not only of our secret acts but of our words, our writings, our responsibility in regard to others, especially the young, the use to which we have put our power over them, those outrages to which society shuts its eyes, that prostitution which trades in bodies and benefits from a tolerance, all those offenses against nature—if we turn the light upon them, the light that came into the world and which the world has not recognized, all this is suddenly revealed as a ravaged world, abysmal, spiritually dead.

Whether it be an illusion or a folly must be settled elsewhere, I am not examining the question here. I say only that this is the crux of the misunderstanding among the survivors, when one of us passes into eternity.

The good and the evil—it is discernment that makes us choose between them, I feel, when confronting death. The Nietzschean upsetting of all values marks the frontier between two kinds of minds, those for whom evil remains evil, no matter if their life be criminal, for whom this is a universe of sin and Grace, a universe of Redemption—and the others, who admit no error other than that which injures the collectivity, and who deny that our actions have any least metaphysical connotation.

We are dealing with two distinct spiritual breeds. Some belong to the first, even when they have been blasphemers and deniers like Rimbaud. To bring them back to the world of Grace it would need but the cry of Une Saison en Enfer: "O purity! Purity! It is this

---

* Matt. 5:48

moment of waking that has given me the vision of purity. Through the spirit one goes to God. O harrowing adversity!"

His last hour was prefigured in this cry. All the more so, for Rimbaud had renounced his human glory and had no other ambition but to be forgotten, since the boy he had been and will eternally be, and whom we cherish, filled him with horror. He had no need, as Gide had, to take into account his eminence, his *persona*. His death concerned no one but him. But the most famous authors die alone, they too, and their last words are heard by no one.

VII

Man and Nature, and Art, and what it should be

Strive as I will, I cannot keep my ship from drifting either toward God or toward death. I would like to find again the current of life, forget my age, but it is impossible: the estuary is too wide and already has some of the characteristics of the ocean. I can see the shores only through a veil of mist. What I still have in common with other men are the seasons, the transition from one to the other, to which I have always so keenly responded. It is the familiar current that I must find again by opening the books I have loved, and thus, in regard to them, pursue a meditation that is peaceful and down to earth.

The forward spring weather invites melancholy. For me, these mild days in February are coins too precious; in Auteuil, they are not legal tender. They merely help me to recompose indefinitely in my mind the Guyenne landscape that I have a tendency to embellish, for surely it is not as luminous as I imagine. The painter or poet sees in his mind's eye the human portion of a landscape, his eternity. Utrillo's painting of the white wall in Montmartre, which he made the 4th of August, 1914, is infinitely more beautiful than the actual wall, if it still exists today.

When, each year, the time comes for me to take the road toward the southwest, the treasure of the summer days will have been squandered in advance. The real springtime, when it appears, will have nothing more to give us. No matter! I can enjoy even a return in winter, even in the icy rain; I will welcome those days with

closed eyes and will find in them my delight. No matter how cold
the hand on our forehead, it is enough that it be a loved hand. Even
a dull and rainy month of March knows some moments of remission: one minute of light glorifies chilled nature.

What I called mild weather and which I so highly prized in
former times I can now easily do without, having reached the age of
contemplation. The picture framed by the open window in the
Malagar drawing-room enchants me even if the rain is streaming on
the still leafless linden-trees and on the ancient roof-tiles—a rose-
pink that is unique in the world for me, a color that has never been
rendered except in words, that supernatural color needed for a roof-
tile. And perhaps toward the end of the rainy afternoon, the rain-
bow, like the one painted by Millet, in the Louvre, will spring from
the hornbeam hedgerows and straddle the terrace.

Fine weather is a prejudice of youth. For an old man, the
weather can be neither fine nor bad; it is the very texture of the
weather that seems priceless, whether brightened by shafts of sunlight or clouded with darkness. Each thread of the tapestry woven
by time is precious, since all the faces that have disappeared from
the earth are projected on it by our memory. But even without any
face projected there, and without any of my dead reappearing there,
it still keeps in my eyes the splendor of being a season of time,
mankind's time, the time in which our destiny will have been experienced and inscribed, among millions of others.

The glass of the magic lantern that Proust describes in the
opening pages of *Du Côté de chez Swann* is the same as those I
loved in my childhood, is still what my memory flashes upon that
backdrop of time past, which blends with the present time in which
I am still whelmed . . . But no longer is it Geneviève de Brabant, or
Riquet à la Houppe, or the Beast or the Beauty whose faces are
discomposed by the folds of the badly hung cloth. That child, that
youngster, that ambitious boy, that young husband—they are I
and not I. O fairy tale, of which we shall have been simultaneously narrator and hero, victim, knight, and dragon monster! And
here again I recall the final words said to me by my old serving
woman, in her patois: *"Cric, crac, mon counte es acabat . . ."* Yes,
my story is ended. But time and the seasons are still there, and
weather that is neither good nor bad. The theatrical lighting
changes according to the laws that remain unknown to us, regulated

forever by someone who pays no attention to the drama each one of us plays. He manipulates the lighting and looks at it, and narrates it, if he is a writer, or with brushes and paint he captures moments and inserts them in eternity.

I listen to the rustling of the rain on the roof-tiles of the house that still shelters me, to which the holidays bring me back; and the weather allotted to me will be fine, even if the first storm of the year, beyond the cypresses over there toward Spain, surges up and opposes a dark brassy thunder-head.

What kind of rediscoveries will there be? *Retrouvailles* is a word in my particular vocabulary, to mark, every year, on the margin of the Holy Days, the contact I make once again with my country house, the welcome I receive from it each time with shades of difference. Sometimes it happens that I rediscover the house as I had imagined it, half awake but still submerged in winter dreams; and only the jonquils and the first lilacs that a faithful hand has placed in vases alter the fragrance of the long ago summer which has remained trapped in the cretonnes.

But sometimes the rediscoveries are disillusioning. This winter the house did not respond to the image I had of it as I drove toward it through all those provinces. Winter is the enemy of these uninhabited houses, venerable antiques whose walls we incautiously perforated for modern plumbing, and this year the frost had burst the pipes. A ceiling had been inundated. Then, the armchairs that had been taken away for reupholstering had not been returned. "I've had enough of this old barracks!" I exclaimed, raising my voice, as if these old walls did not have ears to hear.

Within a day, however, things settled into place. I was no longer aware of the damp stain on the ceiling. Everything had combined—above all, the very genius of the place—to make it correspond once more to my fond image and desires.

But not for long. What is it, please, that now so often troubles my rediscoveries? One morning everything was dreadful once more. Yet the morning was woven of sunlight and mist. And the hornbeam, though still not green, would be so next day, and from one hour to another the poplars are changing. What was wrong? The enchantment no longer worked. The walls, rotted with damp, the subsiding roofs deride the idea I cherish of them and try to convey to others. Things and living creatures are no longer what they were.

The reason for this misery is within me. It is not spiritual but entirely physical. Quite some time ago I found out the very humble causes of my spells of melancholy. I have spent a sleepless night, or have caught a seasonal cold, or have some other upset. The old machine no longer runs smoothly. This being so, let the house and garden not count on me to do marvels! From now on, they will merely share in my own dilapidation.

The house becomes again what in reality it is: something which has endured and continues to endure in relation to the ephemera which, from generation to generation, have been sheltered here for a while. My ancestor, my grandfather, my mother came and went here in this ancient hive like busy bees. Now, who remembers them? That young creature I once was, and whose portrait hangs on the wall, almost as effaced from all memory as they themselves are. Suddenly I realize that one must have a certain audacity to yield to an impression of this kind, already well worn in the time of Ecclesiastes the Preacher. But to feel it is to arouse a horror which retains all its virulence, and the peace and darkness of a silent house where the dead have lived and where we were once a youth of twenty surpasses in tragedy everything that words and music have ever tried to interpret.

What terror! There is nothing if there is no God. For a while (the time of a held breath) I regard the universe emptied of God, the world as it is for such a great number of people. Then suddenly the decayed old house rears blindly above the void, and these folding screens, these coffers, these vases are the flotsam of some obscure shipwreck that no one now remembers. They are like the fossils of pre-human epochs.

Tomorrow morning perhaps, after a quiet night, the raised finger of the day, as Proust said, will appear in the gap of the drawn curtains of my bedroom. The call of that tree-climbing bird which has always been associated with the Easter holidays ever since my childhood will be heard again, both in the garden and in my most distant memory. The house will have found again its enchanted aspect, because the one who casts the spell will have regained his power. The world is endurable only to the extent that we recreate it for ourselves. It is a sterile ocean-depth, for me, as soon as faith departs.

To lose faith would be to lose the world.

Such are the reflections that I pursue during these days when the ancient mechanism of my body does not run smoothly and does not propel the blood needed by me to make the stones and trees of this dwelling place occupy the mind and heart of man.

No, this spring season that I wait for throughout the winter does not always keep the rendezvous I make with it. Holy Week is often chilly and sometimes the shivering garden does not fulfill the charming idea I had of it. But this year everything corresponded to my vision, I realized it the minute I left my car. The lilacs did not yet perfume the drawing-room, but already the bushes were tinged with blue. The sunshine permitted just enough mist to hover so that the visible world could merge with my remembrance of it—and not merely for one afternoon, but for a succession of days, all so immaculate that one day could not be distinguished from another, and it was possible to imagine an eternal present.

What is happiness? Does it exist outside us, independent of our moods? On a morning in spring, when the lilacs lend their perfume to the mist, and above my head a tufted lark launches its three calls, and if it is a Sunday, the bells are faintly clanging in the empty countryside, then everything I see and smell and hear is joy and sweetness. Are not this joy and sweetness within me? And I should also speak of the impalpable purity spread everywhere, the world brimming with innocence. Is that innocence in the eye of the beholder? We are in an epoch when an abomination seems possible: the sudden extermination of the human species. Will the spring survive this? No, of course not, if it merely proceeds from my heart and mind. And the conjunction of warmth and matter that we call Nature, these elements of chance, tinged with green and blue and ochre, what caused them to appear on this planet, among the millions of other planets, what power created this? Perhaps chance alone? And perhaps we are the ones who impose upon all this an order and harmony that are merely the products of our minds? Then what an artist is even the most savage man! And more than artist, a creator: weak, tender, suffering, but with the power to add to his creation this distress that God would not know had He not been incarnated, had He not been a man agonizing in a garden at the time of Passover, at exactly the time of year when I am writing this. And the April night was freezing cold, since Simon-Peter denied Him in the High Priest's courtyard, standing by a fire the soldiers and servants had lighted.

We alone could have introduced into creation the poignant regret of lost childhood, that love and tenderness in which we will never again share, and which for many was perhaps only a thirst that was never quenched.

Were Tristan and Isolde never again to fall silent in the drowsy night, if the bench remained forever empty where they attained that overflowing happiness which cries out for death, if the human couple were to disappear from the world, the night would be nothing but darkness and void. I see what man adds to the night: the sweetest of all things would be horrible without the passion of the human heart. But the limpidity of a spring morning poses another question. We well know that its innocence is not within us. It exists of itself, by itself, but it asks to be expressed.

It asks to be expressed. Here I touch the reason why abstract art is alien to me. I have a deep-seated notion that the world needs us in order to exist, and that human art is the expression of that necessity. This disaccord of an old man with his epoch, this rejection of new times are the phenomena of old age which, long years ago, as a youth, I swore to guard myself against. Obviously I have but poorly guarded myself, for at this last turn in my life I jib at the art of today. The Nature that I have so loved is the sleeping princess who can no longer hope to be rescued from her baleful slumber by a kiss from a painter or poet. Abstract art testifies that man has nothing to say, nothing to express or define when he cuts himself off from the world the child's eyes see . . . But why speak of these things that are important only to me?

I am sitting on a stone bench in the garden, as I write this, surrounded by a vague buzzing and humming. It is midday. The sun is finishing its job of killing the lilacs. Even the birds are no longer active and they sing only in low voices, as if talking to themselves. We have had no rain for seven weeks. The farmers cannot plow, so hard is the ground. Is it April or August? Storm clouds are gathering over toward the sea. And all of a sudden I am again in the heart of a bygone torrid summer, and mortally sad. The adolescent did not transmute into joy all this brightness. The road I am looking at now, the one that climbs a distant hillside, was in that bygone time the very symbol of forbidden flight. The springtime reflects my own peace, the peacefulness of declining years, as formerly the grass-hoppers and crickets of sweltering Augusts shouted toward the azure sky the protests of a young and desperate boy. But this does not answer the question posed: if no human eyes, no human ears perceived anything of the world, would every season have its sin-gular and irreplaceable aspect?

Without the peace, the despair, or the indifference of man-kind, what would remain? Men, for eons, have felled the forests and created this landscape, so that even after their disappearance nature would continue to resemble itself, like those abandoned gardens where the paths become effaced only gradually. But when all trace of humanity shall have disappeared from the earth, at last delivered, neither the sunlight nor the sky will have altered; then a wild beauty will explode, the beauty which the first man knew, and our fathers themselves knew, when the druidic oak ruled the ancient forest. The springtime will remain adorable, without our adoration. This heart whose muffled throbbing I hear within me, along with that faint rumbling of the storm gathering down there toward Spain, this heart is, even so, not entirely wrong, is perhaps not foolish in believ-ing that it is the heart of the world.

Easter receded into the past some time ago. I have returned to the city. Pentecost, which is quite near, will not bring again the rediscoveries of my school days. How I used to love that foretaste of the long summer holidays! For many years the mysterious word "Pentecost" marked for me only those three days, stormy and lumi-nous, spent in the country, in the heart of the young summer, a brief excursion into a nature still steeped in the charm of the spring; but warmth had come, and already the lethargy of summer.

Nature, at this turning point of Pentecost, was not familiar to me as a child; but I possessed her at leisure, still naked and bare, in the indigence of Easter, and would hold her again in my arms at the end of July and throughout torrid August, already wasted and ex-hausted. The three brief days at Pentecost delivered nature over to me only for furtive possession. That youthful and exuberant summer of the last weeks of May, with the meadow grass high and rasping, was never possessed, you might say I never accosted her, even; the classroom window neatly cut out for me her picture.

No spiritual element whatsoever entered into the charm of Pentecost. The enchantment of Christmas was accessible; it was a babe born in a manger, was a child on the knees of his mother, as I was a child on my mother's knees, it was a child I could hold tightly in my arms. The mystery of Easter was spiritual, it united more closely what I already knew or surmised of life with the miracle waited for all winter, the miracle of the resurrected earth. That secret fermentation of life, that blood of Cybele which blued the banks of the stream and appeared in acid green patches through the rough homespun of the dead ferns. And this miracle was not separated in my mind from the story we meditated day after day after day, and which we almost mimed in the liturgy of Holy Week. On the other hand, the historic fact of Pentecost meant nothing to me as a child. If someone had asked me "What is the Holy Ghost?" I would not have dared to reply with "A dove," although that was, basically, what I believed.

I would have been amazed if someone in my childhood had predicted that a time would come when Pentecost would mean more to me than either Christmas or Easter, as being the day when the Christian mystery breaks through, when a portion of the inexpressible and undecipherable secret is communicated to those who are worthy—but is anyone worthy?—to those who have been granted the blessing of being counted among the faithful and who, that day, are rewarded for their fidelity.

On this day of the Love-Feast, the word of St. John, "God is love," manifests itself at each turn of the sublime liturgy, until the most unreasonable of all the mysteries, that of the Holy Trinity, becomes clearer. I do not say becomes explained; but luminous eddies suddenly stir among the shadows of the abyss. No other religious feast does for the worshipper what this one does: it half opens the door behind which he knows he is being waited for. It is the feast of the true worshippers of the Father, the feast of those who "worship Him in spirit and in truth."*

Two sayings of our Lord set down in the Gospels in regard to

---

* John 4:24

the Pentecost offer the singularity of constituting a promise, not for the other world, but for this world, and these two sayings have so often come to my pen that I hesitate to quote them again yet cannot refrain from writing them down once more; on this morning of Pentecost I cannot resist the temptation. Here is the first saying, as St. John reports it: "If a man love me, he will keep my words: and my Father will love him, and we will come unto him, and make our abode with him."* The second saying carries on the thought: "Peace I leave with you, my peace I give unto you; not as the world giveth, give I unto you."**

Peace, here and now; here and now the most hidden depths of our being pervaded with the unfathomable Trinity. We can judge whether that promise has been kept or not. Between those who have left the Church because they felt their expectation was deceived, and the saints who were not deceived but have clung throughout their life to that eternal quarry that the others loosed for a shadow, there is an immense horde of the faithful who, though half deceived, have continued to follow at a distance, never having had the feeling of the presence within them that the Gospels proclaimed. For the promise included the words, "If a man love me . . ." And thereupon we are thrown back to the eternal Jansenist debate: first of all, one must love, but one must be loved in order to love: "He that loveth me not keepeth not my sayings."*** Yes! He would have kept our Lord's saying had he loved Him; he would have been loved had he kept the sayings.

I no longer care to engage in these disputes; anyway, what ear today would be attentive to such things? This generation is not interested in theology; and fundamentally am I any more so? I accept the two sayings, the two promises, without submitting them to the judgment of reason, caring only to know if they have been accomplished in me, if they have been verified by me in my life, if I can testify before mankind that I have not been deceived.

I hear someone saying, "But you, who preach to us as if you knew that peace and shared in it—have you ever renounced the

---

* John 14:23
** John 14:27
*** John 14:24

world for which Christ refused to pray, and have you not, instead, been showered with this world's blessings? Where did you get the privilege of gambling and winning simultaneously on both Time and Eternity?" I am all the more disarmed by the question now that I am reading extracts from the last *Journal* of Soren Kierkegaard, whom Christians of my kind fear, since his vocation was to unmask us. He carries out his terrible vocation so thoroughly that no trace subsists of authentic Christianity where Kierkegaard's eye has rested. One would say that he had read across the gulf of years this meditation that I am writing, and that he was thinking of me, that day in May, 1854, when he wrote: "What abomination, those millions of men who play at being Christians, who celebrate the Pentecost . . ."

I play at Christianity, I celebrate the Pentecost, and knowing and confessing it, I also confess that Kierkegaard's malediction disturbs me only very superficially. At heart I remain as peaceful as was that man born blind or that leper or the first paralytic whose sins were remitted. Kierkegaard can do nothing against this certitude in me: the human being is loved by God as he is, in spite of what he is, because of what he tries to be and aspires to be. And were only an ounce of love to enter into all these speeches and all this literature, that minimal amount would serve to make man be undeceived by God and God undeceived by man.

Kierkegaard's strange vocation was to strip the faithful of the illusion of being Christians. In this respect he is in accord with Port-Royal, where he would have found his true family. His criticism concerns me and does not affect me. I have been invited to the wedding feast, I am a friend of the bridegroom, there's no need to interrogate me on all the rest.

Now let me take up one by one all the sayings of Jesus which accompany those I have already quoted. He said: "I will not leave you comfortless."* And it is true I have not been left uncomforted. He said: "He that loveth me shall be loved of my Father, and I will love him, and will manifest myself to him."** Unlike Kierkegaard, the Lord does not pick and choose, He does not look for true and false among His followers, but sees a host of pathetic souls gathered

---

* John 14:18
** John 14:21

together from all parts of the world, purified of their defilements, and who call upon Him in the words murmured in church this morning of Pentecost; I heard them: *"O, come, thou Father of the poor . . . O thou of comforters the best . . . Rest art thou in our toil, most sweet Refreshment in the noonday heat, and solace in our grief."*°°° These are the names of that holy dove whose motionless flight in the azure sky of early summer was contemplated by that little boy I was.

°°° Missal, p. 490

VIII

The Nostalgia for Youth, what it signifies

Mystery surrounds those days between spring and summer, for at that time of year I seem to be doomed never to experience them in the country. I am now compelled to spend that time in Paris, just as, in my boyhood, I had to be penned up in school. Without the brief holidays at Pentecost, I would have no idea of what those days were like.

Spring is a short season in Guyenne. The last nightingale had not finished singing when the lethargy of the warm days had already stupefied us. In the classroom, our clammy hands lingered over unfinished lessons. Nothing in the books, nothing the schoolmaster said or wrote on the blackboard with a screech of chalk had as much importance as the bumble-bee that blundered into everything, endlessly seeking the open window and, finding it at last, was sucked out into the blue.

This premature summer weather, in collusion with the young bodies flopped down at their desks, did not raise up a race of fighters; I doubt that any of us, in our school, would have been capable of winning any kind of reward in the competitive examinations. Was there ever a single prize-winner? As for the pupils in the town where I was born, I do not know whether they have often triumphed, but am inclined to doubt it. Not that the tribe to which I belong is any stupider than another, but the languor of the summer made our minds sluggish, and the pupils at the lycées were not spared the affliction.

(75

It is true that Bordeaux, in those times, had only two lycées in the center of town, and they were less propitious for day-dreaming than was our lycée at Caudéran, a suburban settlement, where we breathed the nearby country air and felt its call through the green branches. By its mere fragrance, the earth enticed, from a distance, the young and restless males imprisoned in the classrooms.

In the upper forms, some of the older boys were already passing round "girl-photos." A circus dancer, Jeanne Fabri (fancy my remembering that name!), obsessed the minds of the more dashing young fellows. As for me, I would be hard put to describe the image I had of the human female at that time—perhaps it was that chimera of marble which stood on the public square of Bordeaux; it was a woman, yet not a woman, and was caressed by a little boy's hand.

No, there was something else. No charming monster could have reproduced the indistinct features of the adored creature who called to me through the branches; and when suddenly the harsh voice of the teacher barked out my name with a "Continue!" I subsided on my bench like a bird struck in full flight. "I wasn't paying attention . . ." The yawning gulf of the years that separates me from such an incident does not prevent me from still feeling the distress of a schoolboy suddenly wakened from his dream of happiness. Which means that nothing has very much changed. We are still shut into a classroom. What is the Académie Française if not a school class? There is a chair, and a schoolmaster who teaches the lesson, and dictionaries the pupils consult. The life of a mature man remains that of a schoolboy; he wears a cross like the one that was attached to our black sateen pinafore, he wins prizes, is involved in a whole system of emulation and rewards.

But the voice we hear today is not the same as the voice which made us look up from *De Viris illustribus*. Today, the youthful summer can suddenly appear, framed by the window, but the flashing arrow she darts at us is barely felt on our old hands. Yet we are still alien to the class and its monotonous hum; as in bygone days, our whole being is turned toward that azure framed by the window, toward that infinite void which has become an imminent reality, in fact, the unique reality.

The Nostalgia for Youth, what it signifies

We were lured away from our schoolboy existence by life; today we are lured by death. That is the only difference. An old man beside himself, literally, as was the youth. But the bumble-bee that banged against the classroom walls and then vanished into the blue —it is no longer with that blue sky that he merges. An abyss will swallow him up. What lies beyond the vast spaces? What is that light no mortal eye reflects? The beings I loved when perishable, will I recognize them, incorruptible? Those that I loved when ephemeral, what will they be to us in their immortality? That love which was finally possessed, what portion of it will be left, and what will remain of the sentiment we called love when we loved? Is not human tenderness bound to the poor body, to the heart of flesh, to these mortal remains so soon devoured?

To have faith is not necessarily to believe that there exists a semblance of continuity between what we call life and the eternal contemplation. Although I recall having had a foretaste of it. At certain moments the other world spills over into our world; a loved one who is dead breathes close to us, we have only to stretch out a hand . . . At such times we are as if intoxicated by this evidence: there is no other life, there is but one life, and it will never come to an end. But more often it happens that this gulf yawns before my mind's eye, the gulf spoken of in the Gospel of St. Luke, which tells the story of the beggar Lazarus: "And beside all this, between us and you there is a great gulf fixed: so that they which would pass from hence to you cannot; neither can they pass to us, that would come from thence."*

That open schoolroom window of sixty years ago enchanted one of my readers. His letter on the subject shows, I believe, that he is destined for a literary career.

The tide of letters and manuscripts that floods my writing table every day when the post is delivered taught me very early not to have great expectations. Has a bottle cast into the sea ever brought us a message from a stranded genius? I have no doubt that "mute and inglorious Miltons" are more numerous than those who express themselves. As La Bruyère said, "How many admirable men

---

* Luke 16:26

there are in the world whom we will never know!" It is as true today as in La Bruyère's time. The characteristic of the unknown or unrecognized genius is self-doubt, and the inclination to remain silent, out of pride or contempt.

Well, one morning last month I had, at the very sight of an anonymous letter that turned up in my mail, a premonitory shock, the presentiment that for once a treasure might be floating to the surface. One must admit that an anonymous letter fifty pages long, written in a close-set, compact hand on both sides of the paper, without paragraphs but very legible, like the writing of a studious child, or rather a child who takes physical delight in producing the written word, yes, one must admit, this was rather sensational. I surmised that at last I held in my hand not so much a fragment of a finished work as matter still in fusion. How was I to put that young man on guard against an excess of hope? His is a sick mind, and he cherishes his sickness, for he does not separate it from his essential being, and this to such an extent that, according to him, any cure would destroy his integrity. Thus, from the very start, he poses the problem of Nerval, of Rimbaud, or that Artaud he venerates: he, too, has chosen to be a "seer."

My normal preference for a concise style and for shortcuts is succumbing, I see, to the contagion of the disease which afflicts my young correspondent, to the ratiocinating demon that possesses him and has dictated those fifty pages. For here I am, turning in my tracks with that letter, not sure what path to take and follow. Obviously, I should not fight the current but drift with it, follow this young man's thought which breaks constantly like waves against the same reef, take on the to and fro movement of his suffering, a suffering that makes this twenty-two year old believe he has glimpsed the equivalent in me, so that despite the gulf of time that separates us, he believes he has found in me his spiritual counterpart.

I have met him. And now I must say that our encounter in no way taught me any more about him than had his letter. He is incurable; he cherishes his sickness as being the best part of himself. The disturbing thing is that he may not be wrong. He would be wrong to let his life remain sterile and consume itself, a disaster for his family and for himself. He would be right if he finally produced a work that would justify the choice made by this young night-owl who sleeps through the day, wakes at twilight, and writes all night long till dawn.

That reef against which his thought tirelessly beats offers nothing strange; it is found in all lives, but it is something that most men surmount or circumvent. It remains at the center of our destiny, without altering our destiny. My young man differs from us at this point. This sickness common to all paralyzes him, shuts him into his room, just as hay fever shut Proust into his; but Proust had friends, although he affected not to believe in friendship; he liked human beings, he suffered through them, while my young man, preposterously solitary, aspires to make no human contact except through books of poetry by poets to whom he feels akin.

The anguish which is his sickness and separates him from mankind is more common than he imagines, even at his age. Through what I am writing in my declining years he quite rightly perceived a secret inclination to which I have not succumbed, and which is precisely his inclination. When I had barely emerged from boyhood, I was already regretting—at the age of twenty—my years of adolescence. But this was a source of inspiration to me, and not, as with my young anonymous correspondent, a sickness that immobilizes and petrifies.

I proposed, for the meditation of my young man, a declaration Rainer Maria Rilke made one day in 1911, in a letter to Marie de La Tour et Taxis: "I mistrust more and more this monster that I am, a monster who has never taken an interest in anyone in the constant and torturing way that he is interested in himself . . ." It would serve no purpose to add, with Rilke, that a preoccupation of this kind makes it impossible for anyone who succumbs to it to contemplate the struggles of other men and thus write novels. This consequence of his sickness frightens him so little that he has already consented to it in his heart. He aspires only to write, but not a novel, not the story of another which would distract him from himself—that seems inconceivable to him and literally fills him with horror. Let him realize that this is his sickness, and not, as he persuades himself and tries to persuade me, that he is inconsolable at the age of twenty-two for no longer being seventeen. He is a monster in his own eyes, not because he is interested in no one but himself—and in that respect he is indeed a monster—but because the young man he has become is fascinated by the adolescent he no longer is.

Now, nothing is more common than this. It is the process of growing old, and not old age, that makes us suffer as soon as we become conscious of the fact, when we are no longer children.

That such a thing does not become an obsession with most men, as it has become with my correspondent, in no way alters the fact that many if not all men have felt it. Thus, I myself gave this title to a collection of my poems: *L'Adieu à l'Adolescence.* I can measure far better today the extent of that suffering over growing old, since I have entered into veritable old age, going deeper and deeper into that dark forest which becomes darker day by day and almost hour by hour. There reigns in it a peace I did not know in those times when this forest was still beyond me, when I saw the redoubtable edge of it drawing near; and already its shadow extended over me, but I still had a short way to go before reaching the first trees. I advanced only with my head turned toward that half obscured sunlight, which burned me with a final shaft.

Authentic old age has cured me of this sickness, but in the way that death cures us of life. Death, the thought of death . . . My young man is not ignorant of the fact that his despair over no longer being seventeen, of no longer being the angelic creature who is neither child nor man, arises from the horror which is the least singular in the world: the certitude that everything will end for him, and also that it has already begun to end.

You are not as strange as you think, young man: this fascination of the ineluctable end does not make you different from the common run of men. But the idea of death is never masked for you by another creature, by someone adored. How strange! How strange that the flame which scorifies you without destroying you has not been made to shed a light upon another creature of flesh and blood . . . unless perhaps . . . ? Did such a thing never happen, and precisely during that seventeenth year you so constantly and fiercely mourn? I imagine that a disciple of Freud would be able to pull out of this cavern some small reptile; but I am not that disciple, and you do not want to be cured—that is to say, you do not want to lose what, in your eyes, makes you a unique human being.

The Nostalgia for Youth, what it signifies

I cup your head in my two hands to oblige you to focus your nocturnal eyes upon that most sullied and besmirched word which is, however, the very name of God: love. God is love. I know that you are alien to the faith, for otherwise you would be something different from the sick person you are. However, I ask you to accept as a hypothesis St. John's affirmation: "God is love." If God is love, man is, likewise, and if he loves no other, then he loves himself. But self-love is folly, and it leads directly to "errors strange and sad."

Between human love of the most carnal kind and the love of God in His creature and the love of the creature in God, is the Jacob's ladder at the foot of which you are crouching, your chin on your knees, your arms clasping your legs (that is the way I visualize you), your eyes fixed on that portion of the river bank you have left and will never pass again, you are staring at that beardless face that was reflected in the river at that time and place.

This landmark makes you conscious at every moment that every step you take leads you toward death. The remedy for your condition would be, if you wished to resort to it, the desire in you to love. That would be enough for you to cease being what you are. But I realize that what you are makes the very idea of love intolerable.

No. Being cured is not what is important to you, but what would be important is for you to approach, with the written word, the child you are leaving behind you minute by minute. This return upstream is at every moment more and more difficult, it requires you to arrest all life around you. Then it remains for you to pin down your torment in writing, but you must write about yourself without the least fictional disguise. What other way out of your prison cell remains? Then I must encourage you to work that mine, explore that wealth within you, following through until you reach that boy of seventeen.

Who was he? I was mistaken just now when I implied that almost all of us have been under that same spell. In truth, it affects only a certain breed. The most common adolescent is anxious to become a man and play a man's role; he is not pleased with himself as he is. What, then, happened to you? Were you especially sensitive to the grace of your youth, or did you yield to some obscure repulsion toward the adult you were on the point of becoming? As a matter of fact, it is at this confluence of a repugnance and an enchantment that your sickness began. Your sickness—but perhaps also your *oeuvre*, which could give the clue to the riddle you alone possess. It would be useless for me to seek the reasons for the attraction and the disgust which paralyze you, holding you motionless as if petrified, conscious at every instant of an eternal flow of time; you must express this horror in words. There was that fixed point, that place on the river bank which was passed forever; there was that ineffable ray of light on a boy's face. Nothing in the world exists for you but childhood and death.

Your folly resides in not being able to divert your mind from this. Your insanity is not that of the man, insane according to Pascal, the only reasonable man, who was unable to remain alone in a room. Your folly resides in not being able to leave the room. It remains for you to recite with Pascal "the prayer for the treatment of sicknesses," the prayer for the treatment of folly. Am I right to urge you thus toward your inclination? Am I saying this to help you, as I believe? Would I pretend not to know what signifies this nostalgia for youth? I know what it signifies. But were I to tell you, you would not believe me. It is the arrow indicating the true direction, not toward a marvel destroyed, which will exist no more except in memory, but toward the simplicity of "little children" that Christ recommended to his followers, who can experience it here and now.

IX

On Social Injustice

We do not feel the abrasion of time at every moment of our declining years. Some mornings I wake up feeling so well that I am amazed; it is as if sleep had taken me back to my youth and set me down on a shore I left behind me many years ago, a shore that no longer exists except in my recollections.

I have no pains. I lie calmly in bed listening to the steady rain pelting the windows, the guttering of the eaves, the throbbing of my tireless heart. What peace! Enough to make one believe that it springs from a state of Grace. But does a physical state of Grace exist? The saints did not think so, they yearned to live and die crucified.

Bad weather no longer exists for me. If chagrin should seize me, it would not occur because of this rainy August. However, I realize that my momentary equilibrium will soon be broken. Scarcely has the day begun, when a trifle opens a breach and the flood of anguish filters through, spreads everywhere, and rises to cover everything. I pace back and forth in the room from one streaming window to another. The storm rumbles faintly in the distance. Summer, this year, will exist only in the images I have kept of the sultry Augusts of the past. Not that I dislike these days when the rain keeps me shut in with my books and obliges me to examine them. What prisoner does not talk to his guardians? I open a book by chance: it is Malraux's *Man's Hope*.

I never reread contemporary writers, but it sometimes happens that I will pick up one of their works and test it for its wearing qualities, just as I might handle a fabric to judge its strength. This time I do not dream of weighing what remains of the book I have opened. A witness surges up from the depths of that quarter of a century which, for the blood unjustly shed, caps all other periods of history. I had forgotten that Malraux touches that wound in Spanish Catholicism with a respectful hand, as if he himself were concerned over the atrocious ambiguity. I dip into the book here and there and fall upon the vivid depiction of those *milicianos* shot in Toledo. Here Malraux rejoins Goya.

The Spanish Civil War . . . I must have lived it in a depth that I alone can plumb. The entire tragedy of Catholicism was involved in it. I have not confided to anyone my fundamental thinking on this subject, and never will.

Scarcely had the last common grave in Spain been filled, scarcely had Paul Claudel finished writing his poem in which he opens heaven only to the Fascist victims and the immolated priests (provided they were not Basques), without any allusion whatsoever to the hundreds of thousands of lamentable victims assassinated and pulverized at Guernica and elsewhere by the Nazi bombing planes, scarcely did order reign in Madrid, when Hitler took over.

At that time, twelve million Jews were still alive. Children played in doorways around their mothers, children destined for the greatest massacre of the innocents ever registered in history—more than a million.

Murder reigned over the world as it had never reigned. In Hiroshima, in Nagasaki, humanity took cognizance of the power it held to destroy itself and the planet. When those that were hanged at Nuremberg had been cut down from their scaffold . . . I stop myself here. I was only showing the processes of anguished thought in an old man who, upon waking, was surprised to feel so tranquil at the threshold of a summer day, then picked up and opened Malraux's book, *Man's Hope*.

I fancy I see my readers smile and hear them say, with a shrug, "All the same, you feasted on life, you didn't miss a single mouthful, did you?" I have no reply to make, and this is a problem all-important to the Christian. To believe is to consent to hold firmly the two ideas that seemingly conflict: God is love, and the evil in the world is indisputable. The minute a theologian, even a Thomist, brings me his solution to the problem, I feel secretly inclined to refer him to all those martyrs of history who have been burned at the stake.

As for the reply I give to myself: it is contained in that letter X, that unknown quantity which needs only to be stood up and it becomes the cross—the cross on which our Saviour died, but also, before Him, the cross, multiplied, to which millions of slaves had died, and after Him millions of others. Simone Weil has made me see them. The cross explains nothing, it is merely a sign, a correspondence. It exists, merely. A name, the face of a tortured one, a sad and passionate gaze fixed on us until we pronounce a word or heave a sigh; nothing more to expect. But then the reply comes.

It is not the same for everyone, a single word is said for each of us and it is incommunicable. The Gospel was announced to all mankind, for there is no one, even the farthest removed from faith, the most hostile and indifferent, who has not been touched by that message at some moment in his life. The message may have been distorted, but it remains alive in the depths of the very doctrines that deny it. How many people are Christians without being aware of it! The depression felt on a rainy afternoon in August, after reading some pages of Malraux, becomes transformed for me into this evidence, this joy.

Malraux . . . What has history added to the excitable young man I knew during the 1920's? Malraux a Minister of State! His accession to the affairs of state neither aggrandizes nor diminishes him. It renews interest in him through the questions the spectator asks; but the drama here is no longer that of France merged with the destiny of a man, as it is merged with Charles de Gaulle; it concerns only Malraux's destiny.

History has little to do with the adventurous story of this frenetic genius whose soaring career we have followed since his youth, from book to book, and from one peril to another. He is almost the only writer among us who has not been content merely to write, but has also acted for a cause. For a cause, yes, but mainly to add one more trait to his character, for his own life is what fundamentally concerns him—as was the case with Chateaubriand. And always, he has taken an unexpected direction, as if what determined his course had nothing to do with logical reasoning, but instead resulted from chance encounters—with T. E. Lawrence, through his books, and with General de Gaulle, in person. Basically Malraux is a power-hungry man; and destiny has given him a poor bone to chew on, a ministry to satisfy his hunger! All the same, Malraux, who does not believe in God, ends up by returning, between two chapters of his biography, to the sole reality for him, that one thing which remains of man briefly, fixed on canvas or stone, that part of man over which death has no power: the masterpieces of art.

Yes, I know, there enters into the composition of this life an element of bluff which at times we find a little too painful.

What do they mean to each other, Charles de Gaulle and André Malraux? I can more easily see what de Gaulle is for Malraux than what Malraux is for de Gaulle. But that de Gaulle is satisfied with Malraux, as he surely is, indicates the presence in this great chief of state that grain of folly present in every genius. It may be this grain of folly that takes him out of the stereotype class of statesmen, and may explain why, no matter what he does, even when quite reasonable, he is always rather mistrusted by diplomats of the classic type.

"I certainly know what Poincaré would have said if I had indulged in remarks such as Malraux's," Léon Berard confided to me one day, "he would have sacked me and sent me back to my native Béarn!"

Perhaps Malraux, with his extreme Left background in politics and as a former combatant in the International Brigades, stands at the side of Charles de Gaulle as a reminder of the revolutionary aspect of France. Then too, General de Gaulle himself may be classed as an adventurer, in the most heroic sense of the word. His adventure began a thousand years ago, it does not merely encompass the span of one man's life, the interval between birth and death, as Malraux's does. France has a calling, a mission in the world, and de Gaulle identifies himself with it. France may fail to carry out her mission, may avoid it, but this does not matter; the vocation is there, and de Gaulle assumes the responsibility. Malraux merely composes his own life story between the void from which he came and the void into which death will precipitate him; de Gaulle's life story is incrusted in human history.

Some interesting questions arise. Who knows but what Malraux's association with this leader of men may not finally affect his thought and, more importantly, modify the apparent course of his life and his idea of God? Perhaps de Gaulle, in his lifetime, will manage to clarify Malraux as to the meaning of art, that witness to man's adventure on earth, man, the only animal conscious of his mortality; perhaps he will clarify him as to the meaning of that love which engendered him, that mercy which redeemed him, that light blazing eternally?

"There was that secret," Malraux once wrote, "which did not come merely from death, was much less a part of death than of life, a secret which would not have been less poignant had man been immortal."

What is this secret that Malraux has always confronted beyond the absurd in which the writers of the succeeding generation have immobilized themselves? In this courageous confrontation lies Malraux's grandeur. The metaphysical anguish in him avoids all imposture. The authentic quality of Malraux resides in this contemplation of the void from which adventure does not deliver him. And his weakness lies (at certain periods of his life, but not during the Spanish Civil War or in his combats on the Rhine) in the disproportion in his writings between the admirable word and the arguable political act. With de Gaulle, on the other hand, the style is always the man and the man is always equal to his destiny.

We should follow this idea through. What I am trying to say constitutes great praise for Malraux. His will to power was doomed to be realized in a way not commensurate with his talent as a writer; being Minister of Information adds nothing to his stature. On the other hand, the will to power of a Charles de Gaulle merges with that of the nation, is to some extent absorbed by the will of France to remain a sovereign state.

For my part, I confess it gives me pleasure to contemplate these two men from a distance. And I feel, at my age, the rather childish satisfaction expressed by the novelist Philippe Sollers, who wrote to me, at the age of twenty, "De Gaulle and Malraux—that's romanticism in power!"

But that romanticism should be confounded with history is not very reassuring. The presentation of the drama terrifies us from the moment when the sounds behind the scenes are no longer imitated but are real. The trap into which Père Ubu hurls the good people seemed at one point to be opening beneath our feet. Brainwashing is no longer a laughing matter. What can the hero do against the brainwashers? What can one man alone do? No longer is this a theme for abstract debate. Our life is at stake, and more than life: a certain idea we have of the man born Christian and French, and without this heritage there is nothing to prefer but sleep and death.

Thus meditating on Malraux's *L'Espoir*, I suddenly had the idea of making a study of the great French writers who have dabbled in politics. From Malraux I would have to go back to Barrès, then to Benjamin Constant, then to Chateaubriand. Among the many books I opened and shut during this rainy afternoon in August, I happened to fall precisely on the original edition of Chateaubriand's pamphlet on Bonaparte. Entitled *De Buonaparte et des Bourbons,* it was published in 1814 by the brothers Mame, rue du Pot-de-Fer, and subtitled, *"Et de la nécessité de se rallier à nos princes légitimes pour le bonheur de la France et celui de l'Europe."* The necessity to rally round our legitimate princes for the welfare of France and Europe!

Never has bad faith ridden on such a high horse. Heaven knows that a very small part of me yields to the charm of the Emperor. But most of the jibes Chateaubriand hurls at Napoleon could easily be turned against the king of France who succeeded him. To begin with, and without even opening the book, note the insult that blazes in the very title. The spelling of the name as "Buonaparte" announces the main accusation Chateaubriand emphasizes from the very first pages. Napoleon Bonaparte did not even have the right to a French name! His parents had been Corsicans under the rule of Genoa. As if the blood of the Médicis had not flowed in the veins of the Valois and the Bourbons! As if Marie-Antoinette was the only queen of France to merit the appellation of Austrian! As if Spain and Germany had not collaborated in the procreation of almost all of our Dauphins! And this did not prevent our kings from being, almost all of them, good kings; and they were not always ill served, and France with them, by foreigners that their Italian mothers had brought along in their train . . .

But what gives me pause, beginning on page 3, is a sentence dealing with the great days of the Revolution: "Then out of their lairs came all these half naked kings, filthy and brutalized by poverty, disfigured and deformed by their labors, having for sole virtue the insolence of their misery and the pride of their rags and tatters."

What a sentence! One can go on forever squeezing out its juices. No matter from what point of view we take it, the sentence denounces the crime of poverty. "Their lairs . . ." So, this has to do with wild beasts? "Half naked . . ." Then, not only were they without a roof over their heads, they lacked even clothing to cover them! "Filthy, brutalized . . ." Why, just look at those wicked people! And "deformed by their labors," besides. What labors was Chateaubriand thinking about here? Anyway, they were literally *les misérables*, and in both senses of the word, sneaks and paupers, which well betrays the idea most people have of indigence. Oh! In 1814, we are still far from the prostitute-with-heart-of-gold and the saintly-convict—also far from the cult of the working class which was about to begin, along with the industries that would make it appear as exploited, disarmed, handed over to the risks of unemployment and hunger.

Not one word here that does not turn against the régime Chateaubriand is praising to the skies, although he is a thousand miles from realizing this. He does not ask himself "Why and how, in the richest and most civilized nation of the world, in the Paris of that brilliant century when the aristocracy of birth and the aristocracy of the mind combined to constitute an exquisite élite, such as never existed anywhere at any time, why and how were such great masses of people submerged in brutish poverty?"

The Vicomte de Chateaubriand does not dream of seeking reasons for this, as did so many men of his generation and the generation that followed. Nor does he realize that it is not very smart of him to reproach for their ugliness and wounds those poor devils whose labors had assured such splendid leisure for the charming society of the élite. True, he was to pay dearly for his obtuseness.

Thirty-four years later, when at the height of his fame and approaching the end of his life, would Chateaubriand have been embarrassed had someone shown him that sentence he had written in 1814 with which we are shaming him today? Perhaps he would

(89

have smiled at it at a time when Lamartine, "that big booby," as he called him, was triumphing in politics. Perhaps he would have sung one of the popular refrains of the time:

Chapeau bas devant la casquette!
A genoux devant l'ouvrier! *

But his blasphemy of 1814 against the working class would have appeared less absurd to him, perhaps, than his dithyramb in honor of the Bourbons, from which I excerpted it; for the aged Chateaubriand no longer believed in monarchy, even when legitimate. He counseled the "high race of kings" to withdraw "into the holy night of the past, with the centuries"—as he was about to do himself.

But even then, disenchanted as he was with the monarchy, he would have been quite incapable of succumbing to the allurements of the Republican insurgents of 1848. Democracy never went to his head as it did with Lamartine and Lamennais. He never believed in the Republic. To his mind it was only the briefest stop-over en route toward a world he alone foresaw, a society in which, as he wrote, "each individual will be no more than a bee in the hive, a wheel in the machine, an atom in an organized matter . . ."

How could the author of the absurd and ferocious statement of 1814 become, in the span of thirty years, this prophet who could see infinitely farther into the future than could his contemporaries who believed they were at the peak of progress? The reason is not hard to find. At the end of his life, completely detached as he was from politics, since he could play no part in public affairs, and indifferent to the crumbling of a world he was about to leave, his view was unclouded by any least personal consideration or any ideological preference. The minute Chateaubriand was no longer personally involved, he had the lucidity that comes with total indifference.

In 1814—and how long ago that is—the ambitious man, after fretting for years, had at last obtained the object of his desire: political power. For him as for Barrès and Malraux later on, litera-

---

* "Doff your hat to the worker's cap!
On your knees to the working chap!"

ture would always be a stop-gap; writing helped him endure his frustrated will-to-power. Fundamentally these poets loved power and nothing else. Barrès, in the Chamber of Deputies, never played a big part. Chateaubriand was another variety of ambitious man. In 1814, he felt he was bound to play a big part in the Restoration of the Bourbons, and was far from realizing that there was not one feature of his personality but what was odious to the gouty king, and had no idea that Louis XVIII would one day write, in regard to him: "Beware of ever letting a poet meddle in your affairs, for he will lose everything. Those kinds of people are good-for-nothings." Chateaubriand's historical study, *De Buonaparte et des Bourbons,* shows it was dictated by all the passions that most surely blind a prophet. Not that he fundamentally hated the vanquished against whom he fought, in words, tooth and nail. Napoleon "with his tyranny, shut him off in another kind of solitude." Napoleon was part and parcel of his, Chateaubriand's, destiny. They made a pair, and each of them was the torch of the other. The antipathy the Vicomte aroused in King Louis XVIII very soon restored his lucidity, for Chateaubriand's lucidity was always in inverse ratio to his political success. He could see more clearly the less he hoped for himself. This is why the year 1814 marks the nadir of his blind infatuation.

What do I care for Chateaubriand and everything that issued from him! I am now resolved not to succumb to the temptation of my first *Mémoires intérieurs,* or musings on my life. The books I have read shall no longer serve me as alibi; no longer will I try to give a distorted reflection of my true image. The childhood that I found again, in those books, was the creation of my mind. Although I will not deny that I was born and raised in an enchanted world. But there are somber enchantments, maleficent gifts, bad fairies that assemble around cradles. I repudiate no one, I bless all those good people who took care of that little boy so easily hurt. All the same, I have spent too much time and derived too much satisfaction in blurring, in effacing, in painting with bright colors what was somber. I have kept silent on unspeakable things. Not that I was trying to preserve my public image, nor even out of shame or modesty—although I have abhorred in others that willingness to reveal all, down to the inmost recesses. If, for the writer, to live long is to have received the grace refused to all the poets who died young,

(91

which is, the chance to complete one's own statue, to give it the final touches, I am aware of the fact that old age has obligations and that I cannot take refuge in the excuse of having been interrupted by death before having had time to divulge everything, that "everything" which is nothing, I am tempted to say, with a shrug. Yet that nothing is the whole of a pitiable life. If I have kept silent and continue to keep silent, it is because the story of my life cannot be detached from an abundant context. I draw along with me a whole breed. I violate a law of the tribe which stated that nothing should be revealed to outsiders. And the fact that almost a century has passed over those minor family dramas does not render me less sacrilegious and perjured in regard to those pitiful dead people whose reproach I have already heard.

> Lorsque la bûche siffle et chante, si le soir,
> Calme, dans le fauteuil je la voyais s'asseoir,
> Si, par une nuit bleue et froide de décembre,
> Je la trouvais tapie en un coin de ma chambre,
> Grave, et venant du fond de son lit éternel
> Couver l'enfant grandi de son oeil maternel,
> Que pourrais-je répondre à cette âme pieuse
> Voyant tomber des pleurs de sa paupière creuse? *

At this point, I stop to interrogate myself, surprised, for I seem to be insinuating that I belong to a singular family, beset by strange fatalities! Nothing could be further from the truth. The history of my family is no different from those that unfolded at the same time in other families of the same class. Nothing happened but the most ordinary. But the atrocious thing is this "ordinary" in life, a peculiar lighting of these respectable and well-to-do bedrooms of bygone times, when someone forgot to lower the wick which blackened the globe and stank. Nothing more happened under this roof

---

* When the log hisses and sings, if at night,
Calm, I saw her seated in the armchair,
If, on a cold blue night in December,
I found her huddled in a corner of my room,
Gazing maternally upon the grownup child,
What could I reply to that pious soul,
Were I to see tears fall from her sunken eyelid?

than happened under the neighbors' roofs. Other secrets, but of the same order. Money was the alloy common to all those human particles. Death dispensed it by the expected heritage, and—yes, I must say it—expected and hoped for, since these "expectations" were what a bride brought with her, and the hopes were linked to the death of a grandparent and also to a mother, a father—oh, as late as possible, certainly, this was quite the way it was understood.

Nothing could be more alike than those bourgeois houses, those private homes, they were as similar as beehives. As to what went on inside them, a portion was known; after which there opened the realm of conjectures, and then the unknown. Scandal or tragedy occurred rarely or almost never—for such things were quickly smothered and covered over.

In fact, nothing happened but sickness and death, in those vast high canopied beds. The comedy ended there, with the foreseen cast of characters. Each one found the attitude and words suitable to the sentiment he should feel—and that he really felt? Perhaps, but at other moments. Like Marcel Proust, who really wept for the first time over the death of his grandmother more than a year after her death.

This was something none of us would have been capable of fathoming at the time. Our small enclosed world did not analyze itself; it believed it was what it seemed to be. The sentiments manifested outside were the only ones that counted, so it believed. For the rest, all that portion hidden and unexpressed was regarded as null and void, it had simply not occurred—except with pious individuals subjected to scruples. What scruples? More often than not they had to do with the flesh and that forbidden region, the things that should not be expressed, and a single thought allowed to dwell there was enough to separate you from God.

But these scruples regarding the most ephemeral reflection, the most fleeting thought about the needs of the flesh were combined with a strange indifference, no, more than indifference, a disregard for the basic teaching of the Gospels: contempt for riches, hatred of money, love for the poor and poverty, the relinquishment of power and worldly possessions; this disregard was both instinctive and voluntary, and it went to such length that far from earnestly desiring to see justice established in the world, such justice (under the name of Socialism) was a threat to inherited and acquired wealth and as such was the absolute evil. If we were to apply Kierkegaard's criticism to this pious milieu and subject it to an implacable analysis, there would not remain at the bottom of the crucible one least particle of Christianity. The strictness in regard to the needs of the flesh gave, in some mysterious way, carte blanche for indulging the passion for property which the bourgeois conscience disguised as a virtue.

Thrift and order were virtues, and one's fundamental duty was to hand down the patrimony intact and, if possible, augmented, it goes without saying. Nothing could be more false than the common saying that wealth does not follow us beyond the grave. How many bourgeois citizens on their deathbed have gloated over having accomplished their recognized mission in the world, which was to transmit the worldly goods they had inherited, those properties which at all cost must be defended and everything allowed, even overt theft, provided the victim was the State, which is to say, the collectivity, other people. Every abuse against the Treasury was allowed in those distant times when the Treasury did not know how to defend itself as it does today. Everything was allowed if it acted against Caesar, because nothing was due to him. This was the unwritten law of the Church herself which the bourgeoisie knew without having to learn it.

When did all this begin to float to the surface of my consciousness? I felt these things before comprehending them. Very early in life I felt and lived them without any clear idea forming in my mind, and long before presuming to judge or condemn. But from this end of the road I have now reached, when I look back, some facts stand out in the darkness, like hard nails, black and gleaming, driven into that enormous accumulation of the years that I have completely forgotten, but those nails remain, I hang on to them, hurt myself, become blood-stained. These were the moments in which the bourgeois and pious child that I was became a man. No, not yet a man. I never was one, completely; rather, a hybrid, divided against itself, already clear-thinking and resolved to remain so, until the day—but exactly when, I cannot be sure—when he realized that his vocation was to maintain a lucidity which was exceptional in his bourgeois milieu and would be manifested one day in his writings.

On Social Injustice

I believe I have never alluded to one of those nails driven into the dark mass of past and gone years. Whether out of timidity, fear, or shame, I have never been able to pin down in words the images I have kept of it. However, the death of my grandmother marked a date in my most secret life; it was a moment of awakening to certain facts of which I had been only vaguely conscious before. It was then that I saw the true faces of people for the first time. The approaching death fluttered the masks on those faces. I was struck by what I saw. But a boy of seventeen, still trammeled in his childhood, does not yield at once to what he sees; he registers it and keeps it in mind.

No memorable incident, however, marked the death of that old lady whose declining years were like all those interminable declines that keep a family hovering in breathless suspense around an armchair, or a bed. Everything said and done in the vicinity of that ruin, in which reposed the patrimony, derived from a liturgy having no relation to the real feelings that I saw exposed when the death agony began.

X

Matriarchies, Patrimonies, Pharisees, Christians

But before going further and committing an injustice, I must call to mind the rules and regulations of this provincial family residing in Bordeaux, while deeply penetrating by one of its roots (the Mauriacs) the sand and gravel of Les Landes and the calcareous clay of the Garonne. Everywhere—in the fields and the town, in our home and its vicinity—matriarchy prevailed. I must go slowly if I am to remain fair-minded when I describe what struck me at the deathbed of my grandmother.

It is easily explained how I came to write the novel, *Genitrix*. Around me, in my childhood, the women of the family reigned supreme. Widowhood had made my grandmother and my mother mistresses of two estates, each one in her House. I regarded those two Houses as the capitals of two powerful domains which did not merge. The bourgeois fortunes which they represented were on a scale that would arouse derision if compared to the millionaire fortunes of today. But those fortunes were solid and well balanced. On the Mauriac side of the family, landed properties predominated; on the maternal side (my mother and my maternal grandmother) there were investments in real estate. The two women controlled these absolutely, along with an important portfolio which would be wiped out a few years later by the Russian securities, doomed to become worthless.

From all I heard said about my father, whom I had never

known, I gathered the idea of a very sensitive man, shy, fond of books, loathing the business affairs which he was condemned to handle. These characteristics endeared him to me. I have no way of knowing whether his young wife had regarded him with pity or some occasional irritation. My grandmother, who was very old, was glad to have this son-in-law act as administrator of her fortune, but under her surveillance. His sole raison d'être was just this: to carry out her orders, with no reward, other than to be, with his family, lodged and cared for by my grandmother—a mother-in-law who was quite affectionate, it is true, but I recall hearing her at table cut short an argument with, "Who is mistress here?" and seeing all present avert their faces and stare silently at their plates.

The fortune had been quite rapidly acquired during the Second Empire by a wholesale merchant spoken of as "a self-made man" whom my grandmother ("of good family") apparently agreed to marry for the sole reason that the old-fashioned sugar refinery owned by her parents in the rue Sainte-Croix was in financial difficulties which were going from bad to worse. I doubt that she was ever pretty. In her extreme old age, she still showed striking remains of ugliness. But it was at that period of my childhood when I knew her and liked her as she was. I even liked the scent of aromatic vinegar I could smell when she pressed me close and gently scolded me. "Oh, the funny little man!" she would say, and "Oh, the little rascal! All men are rascals!" This was a probable allusion to the infidelities of a husband whose commerce in fabrics and shawls took him away from home constantly on long journeys. She also called me "Briscambille!" I like to repeat these words of another century which no one nowadays recalls. Who was Briscambille? I had always thought he was a famous bandit, but the other day my son Claude showed me a book published in 1741 and bearing the title: *Les Pensées facétieuses de Bruscambille, Comédien original*—"The Facetious Thoughts of Bruscambille (or Briscambille), the Witty Comedian." It was a pseudonym of Deslauriers.

Yes, women ruled our households. One of my aunts was still, according to the law, under the control of a husband, but I believe she dominated him. He was an attorney-at-law, was impressively bearded, enjoyed nothing more than to daub canvases, scrape the violin, tinker, and think up puns. He rudely got rid of clients in order to have a little peace.

The one and only time I stayed at the home of that uncle and aunt, during an absence of my mother, I was astounded, one morning, upon entering their room to find them lying in bed together. Nothing I had ever seen was as strange and incongruous as that sight. The long side-whiskers of my uncle, darkly spread out on the white sheets, made it look as though my aunt were lying beside an enormous curry-comb. All the more astounding since that uncle was celebrated in the family for his snoring, which sounded, according to my aunt, "as if he were being strangled." She maintained that her husband's snores could be heard in the street.

Everywhere in my milieu a *genetrix,* sweet and terrible, held the reins, exercised power. The daughter of one of our neighbors had been betrothed to a young man who was very rich but puny, and I overheard my mother musingly comment, "Of what use is a husband like that? He might as well be strung up by the foot-strap of his trousers, on the window hasp."

In my novel, *Le Mystère Frontenac,* I have drawn a fond portrait of our legal guardian. He was our paternal uncle and a magistrate. Although he visited us every fortnight to oversee our properties, he never managed to restore in me the idea of male superiority which is a man's due. To be sure, he differed with my mother on an essential point: he was irreligious, agnostic, perhaps an atheist, as my father and grandfather had been. However, he did not reveal this in any of his remarks—my mother would not have tolerated such a thing—but he never set foot in a church. When we came home from Mass on Sunday we found him still in bed or else shuffling around in his slippers, smoking cigarettes.

One year, on the 15th of August, we waited for him to accompany us to High Mass, where my mother was to sing the prayer of Elizabeth in *Tannhaüser.* But at the last minute he could not bring himself to go. This under-cover warfare was waged in many French families at that time. My mother worried about the example set us by our uncle, whom she did not much like, but greatly esteemed.

She had no reason to worry. We found it quite natural that Uncle Louis did not go to Mass. Uncle Louis did not go to Mass; our watchdog did not follow the hunt. Uncle Louis belonged to one species, my mother to another. Uncle Louis's behavior needed neither praise nor blame. He did not go to Mass; he smoked cigarettes; he brushed his teeth with a particular toothpaste. The minute the curé appeared at the far end of the driveway, headed in our direction, Uncle Louis "skedaddled," as he put it. He strolled in the woods wearing town clothes, including a bowler hat, passing the time, waiting for the end of the week he devoted to his brother's children. And Uncle Louis did not wait for us to come of age to give us our share of the properties, of which he retained the half.

In our family there was always one old bachelor. The cabriolet of Uncle Martin, who had lived during the reign of Louis-Philippe, was still stored in the coach-house when I was a child. His horse pistols were still lying about. After him, during the Second Empire and the beginning of the Republic, there had been Uncle Lapeyre. Having come to Bordeaux to alter his will in favor of "a bad woman," he died that very night in her arms, struck down by the guardian angel of the family. Our Uncle Louis was the third bachelor of the series. And in my immediate family, one of my brothers who was destined to become a priest already showed, in his boyhood, that he was marked with the sign of celibacy.

I observed several other old bachelors in our clan. Nearly every one of them was under the dominion of an all-powerful genetrix. Uncle Louis had lost his mother. I thought of him as an old orphan and his life seemed to me a bit unreal; he was twice orphaned, deprived not only of his mother but of God, in whom he did not believe. Then, being a bachelor, he was sinning against the matriarchal law of the tribe, for women, even as wives, assumed the role of mother, not only in relation to their children but their husband, likewise. It was against this law that an old bachelor was in rebellion. I often heard it said that our father, when my brothers as children asked the least thing of him, always replied, "You must have mamma's permission."

Although properties, capital, and rents fortified the supreme power of the women, they were not the absolutely necessary condition. One of my great-aunts, a widow and quite poor, whom my grandmother helped out with her subsidies lived in one of those one story houses in Bordeaux called *"échoppe,"* and was waited on by

her four children, two boys and two girls, all four of whom remained unmarried so as to provide for the needs of their genetrix.
The two young men brought her the little they earned. The two
girls, when their service to the old lady was finished, busied themselves with charitable works in the parish. Poor as they were, on
their "at home" day, a maid opened the door. At my grandmother's,
this raised a smile or a shrug, but in fact it was deemed that those
aunts of ours quite properly maintained their rank, and they were
helped to do so. I imagine that my great-aunt received from my
grandmother not a penny more than was necessary, and that behind
that brave façade some painful economies were practiced.

In the domain of my childhood, women either reigned or
served. They were either empresses or slaves . . . Slaves . . . As far
back as I can remember, on both the paternal and the maternal side
of the family, and even in the houses where we no longer lived, there
were servants who lived in: women with their heads so tightly
bound up in kerchiefs that, with their hair concealed, they seemed
to be ageless. Their common trait, as I remember them, was an
unflagging submissiveness in the presence of those human beings
of superior essence, quasi-divine, to which race I belonged. Childhood in no way altered the sacred character of bourgeois birth. In
the infinitely small, everything continued to be as at Versailles,
where the least little scamp of good family was placed infinitely
above old people who in some capacity or other were at his service.
The salaries, in the provinces, were at that time so low that it
was possible to maintain a staff of servants even in residences that
were in the main uninhabited. After my grandfather's death, his vast
establishment, Langon, flanked by its two lodges, ceased to shelter
anyone but his sister, an almost mindless old lady. But the cook, the
coachman, and a maid remained in her service. To be sure, our
Uncle Louis visited her once a month to attend to the properties.
The vast house smelled of succulent foods that were always cooked
in chicken fat, especially the drippings from the chickens roasted on
the spit which turned above a dripping pan placed there to collect
the precious juices, drop by drop.
I can still see, in my mind's eye, those servants with their
meek smiles, especially the servants in Les Landes, where my summer holidays were passed—remote countryside, where the roads,

before the advent of the automobile, were merely wagon tracks leading to the farms on the estate. Nothing had changed since the *Ancien régime.* It was a pool left by the receding tide of the past, the most distant past. I saw women toiling in the fields of rye, women who at twenty-five were already aged. They took pride in never having sat down to eat except at funeral or wedding feasts. It was told of one of my great-grandfathers, who died long before I was born, and who, it is true, had a reputation for meanness, that he could not bear to see a woman-servant sitting down and when he did, he would shout angrily, "Stand up, you good-for-nothing!"

It was women's destiny to serve, when they did not rule. We watched them go by, Sunday evening, on their return from the village, laden with parcels like draft-animals, walking behind the farmer whose arms were empty—not so very different from the Arab women hitched to a cart with the donkeys.

I remember Cadette. She was over eighty years old. Nothing had changed for her since the reign of Louis-Philippe. Her function on earth was to fatten the pig—our pig, for she herself owned nothing—which was sacrificed each year at Christmas, and she wept over the sacrifice every year, much to our amusement. Did she love her own family more than the pig? A grandson who was a seminarian treated her with contempt and disgust: *"Ba te laoué!"* —Go wash yourself!—he would shout at her in her dialect. And, for a fact, she was not only rheumy-eyed but black with dirt. In her youth she had heard the wolves howl. She recalled sitting up nights by the light of crude candles and rushlights. And she remembered eating *"cruchades"*—an old-fashioned pastry made with buckwheat flour. I too remember eating similar cakes, made with the same buckwheat, but kneaded with honey; we called them *"miques"* and they must have been a great delicacy for Cadette in her childhood, in that distant time when the wolves howled.

So this is the way I remember my grandmother, the Queen, and Cadette, the slave. They had no contacts, they did not even know each other, for my maternal grandmother knew nothing about the properties in the moorlands, which came from my father. This old autocrat, my grandmother, dominated three daughters, two sons-in-law, properties, real estate holdings; she was impressive, like an ancient tree blasted by lightning—and indeed, she had once suffered a stroke. The medals that hung from her rosary, the chapel at the

Château Lange, where she managed to hold God at her mercy, all these signs were like the green buoys that mark, on the surface of the sea, the place of a shipwreck: an only and beloved son had been engulfed in evidently frightful circumstances, for the secret was unflinchingly kept by his mother and my aunts. I never knew anything about it, except that the corpse of that only son had floated, one day, to the surface.

The rich old lady, feared and venerated, with that nun who served her, those priest friends who came to sit on the edge of a chair beside her, and a mysterious grief all tended to invest with prestige the power she owed to her fortune. She lived in the obsessing recollection of that son who had entered, by what door she knew not, into eternal life.

And the God my grandmother worshipped was an inexorable God in regard to anything relating to the sins of the flesh.

The saintly women of the family judged everything according to a scale forever fixed. In these matters there was no such thing as a venial sin. But everything could be redeemed. The indulgences —one wonders what notion these women had of them. And that splendid dogma, the Communion of the Saints, did it not, as they understood it, bring into their religious life the concept of banking exchanges, compensations, annulment of debt? I do not know. In fact, I don't remember ever having heard them discuss this subject. Their faith manifested itself less in words than in behavior, unhesitating and irrevocable judgments, based on the scale: mortal sins and venial sins clearly defined according to category and kind, each with its price set for eternity.

There were good books and bad books, good newspapers and bad, Catholic workers and the others. Never did I see these judges hesitate.

All of a sudden I am reminded of one of those ladies. We called her Aunt Blanche, although she was not our aunt, but the aunt of our cousins. She directed the lay order in Bordeaux. Her hair was severely parted in the middle. Her throat was tightly held in a high-necked collar and guimpe. A gold cross glittered on her bosom. Her lips were so thin they seemed to be non-existent. Her eyes were of a porcelain blue. I recognized her the minute I saw the play, *Poil de Carotte:* she was Mme Lepic—at least, physically. For Aunt

Blanche was, perhaps, in her ordinary private life, the best creature in the world.

Incredible that those saintly women had taken literally and in the strict sense the dictum: "Outside the Church, no means of salvation." I remember being disturbed over this when scarcely more than a child. It was one of the first things I questioned, and I was resolved to throw everything overboard rather than adhere to that law. But finally they reassured me: there is the body of the Church and there is her soul. One can belong to the body and not to the soul, but also one can belong to the soul and not to the body. I breathed more freely. Yet in my family this was not easily accepted. The question was decided once for all by the saintly women, and I fear—without being sure—was decided in the most Pharisaical sense. Had they ever read the story of the Good Samaritan? Yes, no doubt. But had they understood it? Had one of their clerical friends ever expounded to them what is written regarding "they that worship him must worship him in spirit and in truth"?* I can vouch for this: old as I am, I do not recall ever having heard in my entire life a sermon preached on this theme in a church, nor did I ever hear this parable commented upon.

What I am sure of is that nothing in the judgment of those women ever indicated that they had the least shadow of doubt touching the use of wealth. Everything written on this subject, and the experience these well-born ladies had of the hidden dramas regarding money in every bourgeois family, all came to naught against a barrage that was invulnerable. That barrage had been erected with the tacit approval of the epoch's clergy: the patrimony was sacred. It was a sacred trust and must be transmitted intact, and if possible augmented, to the children. This constituted the bourgeois duty; any other moral obligation was subordinate, and even the laws of God. A certain form of avarice, under the name of economy, became a virtue. A certain hardness toward mankind assumed the name of prudence. These virtues found their recompense in the possession of the patrimony. In fact, the poor were all too often poor through their own fault. Not that this was ever said outright within my hearing. But the bourgeois morals in that epoch

* John 4:24

were as if steeped in this certitude—a certitude arrived at after the Revolution and the abolition of the privileges of noble birth—that money went to the wisest, the most thrifty and hard working, that is to say, to the most virtuous, who were the cleverest. But cleverness is inculcated in the children of light.

Certainly, we learned to recite "Give lavishly, alms and prayer are sisters." Victor Hugo taught us that when one is rich it is a good idea to have a beggar who can intercede for us in heaven. In our poems, we preferred above everything Guiraud's *Le Petit Savoyard:* "Passerby, I'm cold, deign to succor me/See, the snow is falling, the ground is frozen,/ And I have naught to cover me."

I greatly doubt that there was a single adult in my milieu who was capable of conceiving a world less unjust and of believing such a world possible to achieve—and especially of desiring such a thing. On the other hand, almost all of them feared the achievement of such a world, for we were brought up to think that nothing could be more feared than Socialism. And since Socialists were the sworn enemies of the Church, we did not have to look for any reason to condemn them. The fatal ambiguity which tied Christian faith to the conservation of the *status quo* had trained us since childhood to find, for unavowable and scandalous sentiments, some avowable and even edifying expressions.

I finally realized all this, not unexplainably, at my grandmother's death, an event long waited for but which had, however, come suddenly like a thief in the night, breaking into the monotony of a life so well regulated in every minute that there seemed no opening for an event such as death. But death was there, and was alone able to decompose the mixed-up sentiments of the people surrounding me. I suddenly saw in the eyes of my aunt an undisguised expression of—I dare not say joy, but it was something close to it, and heard an excitement in her voice comparable to what one feels in front of a door kept stubbornly shut for many years when, at last, it suddenly opens. Grief would come later, perhaps; it would surely come one day, but later, not immediately. The excitement showed itself in everyone waiting in the adjacent room, where I also happened to be. Two of my girl cousins became convulsed with giggles. "It's nerves," was the explanation. Was it also nervousness that would presently make us devour our food so hungrily? One of my uncles spoke of a coffer. Should it be opened?

The room where we waited was upholstered in green rep, and it was here that the nun who had been my grandmother's nurse in her last illness had slept—against the rule of the Order, but no rule existed that did not bend for my grandmother. It was also the room where, on Christmas eve, we stood round the crèche. Now the mobilized family was waiting for the long-awaited event, the passing of the ancestress into eternity. Her passing would alter many of their lives. Or rather, what they had dreamed of for so many years would be shared out to them, without changing their lives in any real way. For the portion of the inheritance which they would receive would be transmitted by them, in their turn—except for one property that was to be sold, the Château Lange, a huge estate only seven kilometers from Bordeaux and hemmed in by four roads. Not the least strange characteristic of these people who were in appearance so attached to the acquired fortune was their haste to rid themselves of properties which were earning nothing while being costly to keep up and having become a responsibility and source of worry. Those thrifty bourgeois would throw overboard the most precious possession, precisely out of avarice and thoughtlessness, for one did not need to be a genius to foresee the increment-value of that estate, situated at the very gates of the city. Even as a boy, I was astounded that my mother and aunts could be so short-sighted as to dispose of it.

To escape the giggling girl cousins, I went into the bedroom where my dying grandmother was uttering agonized little groans, unconsciously, for she had lost all contact with reality. A close friend, the Abbé Izans, curé of Saint-Louis, was standing at the bedside and pronouncing in a low voice but with great solemnity, for the benefit of my mother and aunts, a kind of oration on the theme "She was a great soul . . ." I was astounded that my grandmother could have seemed to be a great soul. Well! So that old lady, keeper of the patrimony, surrounded by her daughters and sons-in-law who were always so careful not to displease her in any way, and attended by the nun of a nursing Order who served her night and day as though no other work of mercy could be more agreeable to the Lord, that old lady was "a great soul"? I felt anew the lack of harmony between the old lady I had known and the portrait sketched of her in the precursory funeral oration, precursory, since the groaning, now slow, now precipitate, witnessed that the agony still endured.

This divergence between words and thoughts, between visible gestures and hidden desires, was one of the "sources" of the novels I would eventually write. Perhaps I imagined this? Perhaps I've imagined everything that I believe I am sorting out from all these things past and gone, precisely because I am a novelist. At any rate, the funeral oration delivered at the deathbed of my grandmother by the curé of the Saint-Louis church stirred a doubt in me. The great and saintly soul he evoked within my hearing seemed to me to bear no least resemblance to the pious and tender woman who had embraced me, calling me "Briscambille." But who knows? That funeral oration that I understood as the supreme flattery of the most solemn of the priests who had been associated with my grandmother may have traced the exact portrait of a woman who had existed and whom I had not known. There is no doubt that the Abbé Izans had been closely involved in the tragedies of that life now coming to an end. For him, our grandmother, who had been rather senile during those last months, with her little dog forever on her lap, remained for him the heroine suffering a tragedy of which he was the only one to know all the mysteries. No doubt he knew that this Christian woman had suffered more than an ordinary mother can suffer and knew that her martyrdom resided in the fact that faith adds a terrible note to certain deaths—especially a faith as literal and Spanish as was that of my maternal family.

One imagined the Last Judgment awaiting us beyond the grave as being similar to what we knew of the Assize Court. According to the rating of behavior that had been settled by the women of the family once for all, certain sins admitted of no least attenuating circumstance. None was imaginable at an epoch when Freud had not as yet changed the nature of many sins. In that time and milieu, one had to lose all hope for some of the dead. To die in final impenitence—to use Bourdaloue's expression—was to run the greatest risk possible. The more I think about it the more I am convinced that my grandmother, guided by the curé of Saint-Louis at a certain epoch of her life, must have gone through fire on earth, and her façade of a great bourgeois lady was only a façade. The words of Father Izans could only be understood by the three daughters of the dying woman—but not, perhaps, by the sons-in-law whose alien stock made them unworthy to share the family secrets. My grandmother had been that pierced heart which does not cry aloud and shows no sign of suffering. It was for this reason that Father Izans praised her in her last hour, when she would at last know what had become of her son (for according to her idea she would find him, beyond the grave, exactly as she had known him on earth and would resume relations with him and with the other of her dead, exactly as they had been on earth).

The more I think about it, the more I am persuaded that Kierkegaard was mistaken when he affirmed that in all the pious lives around him there could not be extracted one ounce of authentic Christianity. For me, it is at once a mystery and a certitude that, through all the anthropomorphism and Mariolatry in which our saintly women were steeped, Grace flowed, and even streamed. The sacramental life they followed caused virtues to spring and flourish in the depths of those lives apparently Pharisaical, virtues that extended to immolation, and perhaps a total surrender, even if in a bourgeois and petty way.

How did I keep my faith? How could I, endowed with a sense of humor as I was, and a reader of Anatole France from the age of fifteen, keep my faith in spite of what I saw and heard? I could reply by taking up again, in a new light, my meditation on "What I Believe." I was especially offended by the interdictions against modern literature, which I esteemed above all else.

These interdictions cast a suspicion which could have no least shading for those women who, on principle, lacked culture and who forbade all reading outside the approved list of "good books," rating, as among the great, writers such as Zénaïde Fleuriot, Raoul de Navery, women who would never dream of doubting certain things. I do not recall ever having heard in my family the reading of a great book, even a great religious book. I had to discover everything for myself, through the textbooks and through the anthology collected by the Abbé Ragon. I am none too fond of myself, but by the same token my heart melts when I recall that little boy who, at night, in the study, sat reading over and over, moved to tears, lines such as these:

(107

Pâle étoile du soir, messagère lointaine
Dont le front sort brillant des voiles du couchant ...

To be sure, there were my schoolmasters—or rather, there was one teacher, for it was in the upper form, when I was sixteen, that I finally met the Abbé Péquignot, who loved ideas, as he often repeated, and who seemed to love nothing but ideas. He was emaciated, spectral, and so near-sighted that he was almost blind. No doubt he, too, had discovered, gropingly, those few ideas he called "ideas." Yes, he helped me, but in fact I needed no one, for when barely fifteen I had read Racine's *Andromaque* and *Phèdre* and felt at home in that palace of Butherode where Hermione suffered and in that other palace of Trézène where Phèdre killed what she loved and killed herself.

No, I do not condemn those who made me spend my childhood reading children's books and who struggled to keep shut the gates of the garden of knowledge against the boy I was, not introducing him to any great literature, not even of the inspired kind—I knew nothing of the Bible. And I will tell why I bless them.

XI

I became a controversial Catholic Writer

I discovered everything all by myself. I discovered not only the name of a passion unknown to me, but even the ups and downs of a desire not yet felt by me, or at least not yet centered on a particular person. But the discovery that thrilled me was the muted orchestration a certain style permits a masterly writer; I saw that it was a style the writer must possess for himself, strictly adapted, I already foresaw, not so much to the illustrious passion of a Hermione or a Phèdre, but to the confused magma amassed in the writer from childhood, even a childhood such as mine, which was more than preserved, more than imprisoned, it was bound and gagged . . . Nonetheless the familial censors were unable to put out my eyes or stop my ears, and I had seen and I had heard, no matter how narrow the cage that hemmed me in, I had seen and heard the passion which Racine displayed in an immortal illumination.

Already, at the age of fifteen, I could see Thérèse Desqueyroux suffering and dying, I saw Brigitte Pian deceiving herself and others, and despairing, for there was no way out for them. On the level of literature and art, even before anything had been revealed to me at school, could I remain indifferent to that little world within me, upon which fed, unknown to anyone, a nascent monster, the novelist?

Above all, how could I have turned away from the only open door, the one opening out upon eternity, which is to say, the Catholic faith? True, the approaches seemed to be obstructed, as I said, by the base state of piety. What I once called "the falsehood at the heart of truth" was to be, from my adolescence on, one of the crosses I had to bear. But my faith, my hope, my love emerged fortified by what killed belief in God in so many others subjected to the same disciplines (I am thinking particularly of Simone de Beauvoir). "It's because you were not a philosopher," I am told, "and so, the powers of sentiment overpowered in you a weak and disarmed reasoning." I do not deny it. I am not very proud of this when I compare myself to such and such a one. I know all too well what it is to be cultivated, I have loved all too much true culture in others, so that I would never claim to be cultured myself. If I admire myself it is for having reached this point in my destiny and to have reached it with the means at my disposal. I have known the majority of philosophers only through the comments made on them by those who have read them, and have known foreign literature only in translations.

Certainly, I was a great reader—and during my childhood and early youth, as I clearly showed in my previous *Mémoires intérieurs*. Indeed, I was almost uniquely a reader, and not at all a worker. This may appear almost incredible to those who are impressed by the mass of my complete works. But in fact I have always been the man least accustomed to remain seated at a writing table. I have always set down my thoughts in a notebook resting on my knees. *Thérèse,* that novel still spoken of after forty years, was the work of a few months if not of a few weeks, as were almost all of my other novels.

Publishers have often proposed work to me, of the kind that brought fortunes to my hard-working and well organized colleagues. I have always eluded those tasks, mainly out of a certain indifference to money as soon as I have earned enough to prevent me from having to think about it; but my lack of enthusiasm, my immense capability of withdrawal and day-dreaming—these are the real causes. My *oeuvre* fabricated itself all alone, it swelled like a river that springs from all its affluents, which had their source in circumstances, occasions, the necessities of the writer's craft. My writings have benefited from the fact that, no matter how lazy I was, I always wrote the least article with care, putting my whole soul into it. I will have remained all my life the sixth-form student who wants his essay to be better than all the others and to be read aloud in class.

My example proves that for a writer to leave behind him an *oeuvre* impressive in the number of volumes, it is less necessary for him to be a hard worker than to be a scrupulous writer, careful not to publish his dross. But above all, it is necessary not to die young. The leaves detach themselves and the dry leaves accumulate with the years, and the old oak will put forth new green leaves until the end.

It is not exact to say, however, that these powers of sentiment in the boy that I was met with no least objections of reason. I was not ignorant of the questions that were being asked in cultivated Catholic circles at that time, and I was perhaps better informed than other youths of my generation and was also more preoccupied with them than were others.

On this point, the initiator was not one of my schoolmasters. My professor in the top classical form was the Abbé Péquignot, to whom I owe much, but although he was my confessor for a time, he had no direct influence upon my religious life—yet when André Lacaze and I drew up a list of "intelligent Catholics" his name figured there, between the names of Maurice Blondel and Laberthonnière. That list, I may say, was not a long one; the number of imbeciles seemed to us far greater. "You think everyone is stupid!" my mother said, exasperated. And it was true that André Lacaze and I did find everyone stupid. After I had read *Sous l'Oeil des Barbares*, I adopted with bitter satisfaction this contrary position: I was entrenched on the other side, was cut off from all the others, those barbarians and their "bold, offensive laughter."

André Lacaze was the schoolmate who confronted me—as a seventeen year old philosopher could—with the ideas that Pius X was to condemn under the epithet of Modernism. André was in rebellion, ahead of his time, against the disciplines of a Church to which nothing could have compelled him to submit wholly. Strange! He seemed all the more to rebel in not being able to conceive of any possible life outside the walls of a seminary, and took no least interest in any questions other than those posed by theology or exegesis. You would have said that his indignation, his refusals and disdain needed the strait-jacket he himself later put on when he donned the cassock, as if to experience their torment.

I acquired ideas through André that I would never have picked up alone, from books that were too heavy for the ignorant

(111

schoolboy I was. Thanks to him, I benefited from a kind of vaccine, injected rather early, to immunize a young Christian against all the poisons of knowledge. And at the same time I freed myself, in his company, from the irrepressible anticlericalism imbibed by all Frenchmen, even the pious and highly educated, with their mother's milk—or with their first classical readings (we admire the Pascal of the *Provinciales* no less than the Pascal of the *Pensées*). Had our teachers overheard our remarks, they would have been horrified. But really, the very act of raging and fuming in the defense of Father Loisy and his "Annals of Christian Philosophy" in a college where our classmates were thinking only about the Paris-Madrid race should, on the contrary, have reassured them, at least as far as I was concerned. As for my friend, he was destined for the Church in the way that a young man, simultaneously filled with love and hate, marries a woman he adores but considers idiotic, with the hope of improving her. Ten years later, when he was a seminarian, he lunched with me shortly after my marriage. My young wife, scandalized at some of his remarks, asked him timidly, "Now, really, Father, why did you enter the Church?" And he replied, "To blow it to pieces, Madame!" I was used to André's style, and knew this signified he hoped for great changes in the Church. The changes he dreamed of would seem timid now, compared with what was accomplished before our very eyes by Pope John XXIII, for these reforms surpassed by far everything André had called for at the age of seventeen.

Yes, when I look back on my life I see that the faithful Christian I have remained was immunized from childhood. At first sight it seems amazing that, when I became an author who was known, admired, and discussed, I did not balk at the reputation I was given of being a morbid or even pornographical novelist, a reputation that hounded me from the very beginning of my career, making me very soon mistrusted in Catholic circles. General Castelnau, it seems, once declared, "I would not like to see that man's books in the hands of my children!" *La Revue des Lectures* of Father Bethléem spared not a single one of my works. Even *Asmodée* was, in his opinion, a play which "if absolutely necessary, could at most be seen by very sophisticated adults."

At about this same time, some young Belgian Catholics risked asking me to give a lecture. I was received in a way that really astounded me. The reception they gave me was amicable, yes, but circumspect. A cassock was lurking behind every pillar. Notes were being taken. Henri Davignon introduced me, dissociating himself from my works by saying, "We have invited Monsieur François Mauriac, but not his characters. You are not here, Thérèse Desqueyroux! You are not here, Maria Cross!" There were many other examples of such tact. When it came time for the toasts at the end of the repast which followed, one of my hosts warned me not to say that I felt as though I were in France, since such remarks greatly displeased people in Brussels. I reassured him. "In Brussels," I said, "everything, even the brickbats, astound me!"

If I endured this kind of needling and at no moment was tempted to fire a final round at the bigots or give them one last tongue-lashing before taking to my heels, it is due, I believe, to my having been vaccinated in my childhood against this kind of stupidity. Father Bethléem's censure in the name of *"Oeuvre des bons Livres"* had already circumscribed my reading when my intellectual life had scarcely begun. Certain works of the most anodyne character were marked with an R, which signified they were to be handled with caution. Perhaps the book contained something about love between a man and a woman, or perhaps about a child born out of wedlock? In literature everything good was bad. I realized this was the viewpoint in certain quarters and adapted myself to it in my own way gradually, as reading became my devouring passion.

How did I resist this evidence? The people surrounding me, those saintly women, could only endure falsehoods on that level; they forbade me and forbade themselves everything that expressed life as it is. Never at any moment, thank heaven, did this evidence incite me to question the value of a doctrine which created this state of mind! No doubt, it was this antidote which immunized me to the poison and guarded me against its effects.

Of course I was irritated and indignant, of course I tormented myself. We protested, André and I, that the Lord who preferred above all His other apostles the author of the fourth Gospel had no partiality for the priests of Father Bethléem's stamp. From that point on, we believed in the mind as sanctifying and allinspiring. I had an inkling that poetry is truth in the absolute sense. I kept within me a store of faith, and the writer nourished himself

(113

on it. I believed and fortified myself with what was to plunge André into an exhausting dispute.

True, I was turned aside from the eternal problem by my pursuit of a temporal destiny which was already vaguely shaping up. Without any precise goal, I advanced on a road in a certain direction, a road Bourget and Barrès had traveled before me. Among the living, while I was still a schoolboy, I knew no other masters. André's destiny was different; he would go almost directly from the lycée to the seminary, and no human ambition or pleasure would draw him away from that wrestling with the angel that he would carry on until the end.

When I wrote, in my *Vie de Racine,* that all biographies should pass through ourselves, be our own story, it was literally true as far as I was concerned. I was conquered in advance, as Racine had been; like him, I found myself basically in agreement with my censors, many of whom, for example Jacques Maritain, were far from stupid. It would be easy to find at the heart of every one of my novels written during that period a trace of this conflict and to decipher the ruses I employed to silence the Messieurs Saci and Singlin of my time.

The most astounding thing is that as my religious experience and meditations led me to take a view opposite to the Jansenists on the subjects of Grace and personal responsibility, the more my idea of sin became transformed under the influence of Freud, and I clearly saw (or believed I saw) the human reasons why the Lord said to the woman taken in adultery, "Neither do I condemn thee: go, and sin no more," * and remitted so generously, almost with tender indifference, all the sins of a pitiable life. I nonetheless continued to think according to the ways acquired in my childhood, yielding to the same anxieties, the same qualms, although I was convinced of their folly. The devil finds no better aid than the scruples of a Christian. Their very absurdity incites the person affected to throw everything overboard and sin with a vengeance, in order to reassure himself that he is not worrying over nothing and has reason to torment himself.

---

* John 8:11

I became a controversial Catholic Writer

The strangest thing about a Christian of my kind—and this was true from my early childhood—is that he confuses the love of God with the hidden satisfactions, that possession of the inner man, its invasion by the One only the pure in heart can know. And it takes but a self-satisfied glance, a thought held back and momentarily fondled, to dispel those feelings of holy sweetness, those "adorable ideas." Scruples are an ailment which then becomes a kind of permanent anxiety, a state of alert, as if the pearl of great price mentioned in the Gospels had become the treasure which kept the cobbler from sleeping and singing.

How long ago and far away that bedroom where the agonized groans became weaker and where Father Izans ended in a whisper his funeral oration for my grandmother, yes, and there is a great distance between that bedroom and the Boeuf sur le Toît night-club where, a few years later, very little alcohol would be enough to make me lose my bearings, and where every human countenance would give offense.

XII

The Reckless 1920's, and the Tragic Years 1935–1945

Every countenance, every life would give offense, for I knew every one of their stories, every one of their tragedies. Christian that I was, I still did not believe I belonged to another species. Yes, I was a Christian, was married, was a young father, and had been all this since just before the war. How frightful that world was, following the Armistice, and how could it not have failed to make me live in a kind of terror, since already, before the war, I had not been able to wait any longer to build my nest and be enfolded in a pure love which would defend me against the others and against myself! I was a man of letters, like all those young men of letters. Perhaps I would have been different had I not, I too, gone through four years of anguish, bereavements, horrors, and humiliations on account of my shattered health which classified me as "unfit," leaving me no other part to play than the useless one I played in the ambulance corps at the front. Then suddenly there had been that exodus from the tunnel, and that frenzy to which I only slightly succumbed. But that slight amount was a great deal, was too much, because, for me, it involved the Infinite.

What was for the others only a permissible dissipation was deadly for me; it went to the depths of my spiritual being, the source of true life . . . Oh, perhaps here again I am putting too much emphasis on the sublime. But the sublime was, indeed, involved. One must also take into account the reaction of a bourgeois writer whose work was beginning to be recognized, a writer who had passed his thirtieth year and instinctively felt that the excesses, harmless for his comrades because adapted to their characters, would have thrown him hopelessly out of the path he had traced for himself.

I would not swear that I was fully conscious of this or had formulated a particular idea. I am inclined to believe that religious preoccupations were uppermost in my mind. But how to untangle the skein of causes, reasons, complexes and reflexes? Certain it is that the climate of the 1920's in Parisian bookish circles and society seemed charged with poisons; we felt spiritually "gassed" as we had been physically gassed during the war.

The Christian, even the bad Christian, if he has kept his faith, possesses a sixth sense, an antenna that discerns in those individuals of his circle that fatal malady which spares no one. I did not know that Raymond Radiguet, that marvelous night-owl sitting motionless and unseeing on his bar-stool at the Boeuf sur le Toît, was soon to die. I did not know that Drieu la Rochelle, Jacques Rigaut, René Crevel would kill themselves, but I saw with my spiritual eyes a glimmer, a sign hovering above those charming heads. That boy whose name I have forgotten, with the beauty of a dark angel, I remember watching him one evening as he danced with the marvelous Anne-Marie P . . . , holding her by both hands, and, watching, I sensed a vapor of anguish rising above that delightful couple. He was to be carried off a few days later, fully conscious and screaming with despair, and she was destined to be killed at the wheel of her car.

André Breton was wrong to deny Jean Cocteau the title of Prince of Poets, for he was certainly the prince of that coterie led by the surrealists. Pitch their camp as they would on the wildest of its frontiers and hold in contempt the frivolous Prince, the surrealists were nonetheless dependent upon his rule. Drieu la Rochelle was their friend and maintained a liaison. We met some of them in the "literary salons." I recall meeting Aragon in Mme Lucien Mulhfeld's salon, and hearing René Crevel remark to the dismayed Anna de Noailles, "No, Madame, poetry is not being written today."

But I am not writing the history of that period, or the history of that milieu; I am writing my own story. I recall only the ominous mist that rose from that bacchanal, and I repeat that it is

(117

not surprising that, while remaining a Christian, even when I succumbed to the general madness, I also felt the anguish of the experienced man who is aware that cholera is aboard ship and knows the name of the ship's captain. I have often told myself that the movement of conversions to Catholicism which increased greatly at that time, especially in André Gide's circle, was almost a stampede: Dupouey, Ghéon, Copeau, Du Bos, René Schwob . . . I saw them leave the ship where alcohol and drugs favored *"les erreurs étranges et tristes"* and swim away. What effect would those "sad and strange sins" have on me? Would I recover my senses one day in mid-ocean, cut off forever from God, lost forever?

The survivors of that period will no doubt judge that I am painting the scene in ridiculously dark colors. Then let them read the *Récit secret* of Drieu, or his *Gilles,* or Kessel's tetralogy, *Le Tour du Malheur.* That was the way it was. Not that writers and artists are different from the rest of the human herd. Alcohol, drugs, homosexuality, sadism did not exert more power over them than over others; but these things happen to have been expressed in writing, therefore revealed, and all the teeming horrors in the human slime floated to the surface. The story of Radiguet, the story of Drieu are no different from thousands of others, but they have been told and revealed.

That stampede of converts had repercussions in my soul. Upon reflection, I believe I am wrong when I count a defensive bourgeois reflex as being what restrained me from letting myself be swept away by the current. After forty years, we cannot bring a well-founded judgment to bear upon what we recall of the past. Our recollections no longer spring from within us; we can have no idea of the person we were at that time, a creature who has become alien to us. We can only rely on the written testimonies that creature has left. That thirty year old man who bore the same name as the septuagenarian I am today is known to me mainly through the pages of an essay I wrote, *"Souffrances du Chrétien,"* published in the *Nouvelle Revue Française* at the time. That article testifies to the fact that I was suffering with the anguish of a soul incurably Christian, and I cannot refute that written testimony. Was that cry a heart-rending appeal to God? No, it was rather a cry for help aimed at my fellow-men. And it was heard.

There is a very hidden kind of charity, and it is one from which I have benefited at certain moments in my life: that of friends, known or unknown, who plunge into the water, take hold of you and bring you back to the shore. I recall that in 1910 or 1911, Robert Vallery-Radot literally kidnaped me and set me down in a Dampierre inn. Later, Jacques Maritain never ceased keeping an uneasy and sometimes anxious eye on me. But he did not attempt any direct intervention. He responded publicly to any call for help that escaped me. I had the certitude that he kept watch over my life. At the particular time I am recalling, he was caught off guard, it is true, and the conversion of Cocteau and of Maurice Sachs made me doubt him a little. But it was time, more than time, for help to come: my essay on the sufferings of the Christian echoed the cry of a soul half asphyxiated. And Charles Du Bos, himself only recently converted, realized that not a day must be lost.

To be sure, I knew him; we had struck up an acquaintance. He had devoted an admirable article to my novel *Le Désert de l'Amour* in the *Nouvelle Revue Française*. Following the death of Jacques Rivière, he and Ramon Fernandez were my guardian angels. Perhaps, without them, I might have been cast into the outer darkness of the Boulevard and academism, had there not been someone at the *"N.R.F."* to appreciate a certain tone in my writings and to perceive that a certain question was posed in them. Du Bos realized that the hour had come to give me the answer.

He realized this thanks to our encounter at a moment crucial in both his life and mine. He had just taken the step: he was in the full flush of his return to God and in the excitement of sacramental life found again. He was Polyeucte upon leaving the temple where he planned to overturn the statue of Gide. And I, on the other hand, had sunk to my lowest level and, spiritually, could descend no farther without perishing. But I realized this and suffered. This was what made me so willingly follow the advice of Du Bos, who urged me to entrust myself to Father X, the priest who had rescued him.

This priest was by birth a Jew; he had been converted a few years earlier by the curé of Ars, that person unknown to me who was Father Lamy, parish priest at Courneuve, a veritable saint, through whom he had touched the miraculous. That experience was apparent in the way he said Mass, slowly, in a kind of intimate communion with Christ and with God the Father. An intractable

Thomist, he was the very epitome of what is today called "integrist," a Pharisee and son of a Pharisee, as was St. Paul, priest according to the rule of Melchizedek, *sacerdos magnus* on the frontier of the two Testaments, and he was the priest most apt to succor a lost sheep, exhausted and no longer struggling, wanting nothing more than to be carried helplessly on robust shoulders.

But as the lost sheep recovers his strength, he will not tolerate being carried, as those who have read between the lines of the *Journal* of Charles Du Bos have seen: the lost sheep, at first brimming with admiration and gratitude for the one who rescued him and held him in a strong embrace, soon wants his freedom. Indeed, it is impossible to imagine two natures more opposite than Du Bos and his confessor, who became mine.

Very imprudently, I had created what was to become the instrument of torture for my friend. I had had the baleful idea of founding a Catholic review which I hoped would counterbalance the *"N.R.F."* and constitute a rallying point for the new converts—baleful, because I had closely associated Father X with it. As a matter of fact, he had forced himself upon the project. He considered himself responsible to God and the men of *Vigile*, as our periodical was called. From the first issue on, he blue-penciled, line by line, without any scruples of a literary kind, much to the horror of Du Bos, in whose eyes there was no crime worse than the mutilating of authors' texts.

For my part, I suffered especially at the sight of my friend's mute suffering. I was safer than he from the blue pencil of the intractable priest, who had to respect a little my literary standing and the prestige it gave me. At that time, Du Bos was involved in all kinds of struggles, against poor health, against his destiny as a critic without a rostrum and without readers, as a writer unable to write, able only to dictate, as head of a family—and I have never known a man better organized to ruin his family, so great was his need for the superfluous, for luxury, that he was doomed to end up in destitution. As for *Vigile*, he was forced, under the whip of a merciless torturer, to commit in every issue crimes against literature that he felt dishonored him. He obeyed, and suffered. I very soon realized that what would surely die, slowly asphyxiated by Father X, was *Vigile*, and that we need only wait for the end. Its publisher, Bernard Grasset, upon seeing the magazine on a table at the home

of Arthur Fontaine, exclaimed ironically, "Oh! So YOU are the sub-
scriber to *Vigile!*"

Although we had only four issues to bring out each year, the
censorship practiced by Father X created gaps that we had to fill at
the last minute with whatever we could, and this was most often
furnished by Du Bos himself, with his serialized *Journal.* I was
conscious of my friend's tragedy without being directly affected.
The failure of *Vigile* was compensated in my life by too many
successes for it to cause me any real suffering.

The novelist in me profited by everything that was disap-
pointing in Father X. Not that he ever served me as a prototype. I
owed him too much to allow myself for a moment to portray him,
although at that time I excelled in such portraits. Had I been
tempted to portray him, I would have taken account of the authenticity of his union with God. My faith had become a living faith in
contact with his: this was something acquired forever. He could be
hard to get along with, scarcely endurable for a mind such as mine.
Even so, he remained my rescuer.

And yet I cannot deny it: the novelist in me did profit from
the causes of Du Bos's sufferings. Every Sunday, after the High Mass
at the Benedictine chapel in the rue Monsieur, we met for breakfast
in a neighboring house, at the home of a splendid woman, a sculp-
tress, about whom I still feel remorse over having refused to pose for
the bust she wanted to do of me. Gabriel Marcel, Roland Manuel,
Isabelle Rivière, Georges de Traz, Max Jacob and several others
made up our very singular and fervent group. There were also a few
young girls, among those that Father X steered toward a convent,
for which he was the privileged provider. In his eyes, I imagine, this
was his essential mission; from the viewpoint of the century, he was
a menace to any girl who was handed over to him spiritually. However, I could only admire him for having interpreted literally the
command of our Lord: "Be ye therefore perfect, even as your Father
which is in heaven is perfect." * The souls under his inflexible guid-
ance who were capable of giving all, gave all.

The Sunday Mass in the chapel of the Benedictines of the rue
Monsieur in those years from 1925 to 1930 clearly had a direct effect

---

* Matt. 5:48

upon many artists and writers, and that chapel was an irreplaceable site of God's Grace. This is so clearly evident that I have never understood how the Diocesan authority could have consented to its disappearance. The community that abandoned this post seems to have paid dearly for that abandonment. I doubt that what remains of Christian letters has ever found a fishpond such as that one was. The sacrifice of the Mass was celebrated there as it rarely is elsewhere; I mean to say, without our ever feeling momentarily irritated or scandalized. The Benedictines sang like angels. The voice of the celebrant priest (Father X or Father Zundel) was in harmony with theirs, and his gestures made visible what was invisible. Never has the Presence seemed more real to me than it did in those years.

Thus, Father X never inspired me to do a portrait like that of M. Coûture. Although some of the characteristics of the Pharisee may perhaps derive from him, it goes without saying that this priest who was immersed in the supernatural in no way resembled Brigitte Pian—except, it may be, in one point. He may have furnished me with a fearsome trait; a certain manner I will call "turning the cheek" which he had and which drove me wild. If I had any reproach to make him, if the good priest sometimes scandalized me (and this was not always without cause, in spite of his great virtue, since he had been born and raised a Jew, and his poor health having forbidden the seminary, he had not received the normal formation of a member of the clergy), if, as I say, I sometimes thought I had the right to blame him, far from admitting that he was in any way wrong, he would sigh and murmur, "I knew I must suffer today through you!" And he offered his suffering to God. He made himself a martyr and in so doing made me his torturer. It did no good to protest or to stamp my foot; the more irritated I became, the more he presented himself as a burnt offering. In this respect, there must be no thought of similar traits in Tartuffe, because there was not an ounce of imposture in Father X. He fooled no one but himself and he did this unknowingly.

"The canicule of the truth"—this statement made by Du Bos in regard to Claudel can be applied in quite another sense to this priest who, like St. John, having touched at one instant in his destiny that something which concerned the Word of Life, had been as if dazzled by so much light, and as he saw us poor children still crawling in the mud of our sins, heard the absurdity of our ideas, our belief in progress, he was horrified. But we were neither philosophers nor theologians. What we thought on those subjects, we frivolous men of letters, had no importance to him. If on the other hand he denounced and overwhelmed Father Laberthonnière, for example, it was because he was dealing with a theologian. But he counted it of little importance when a novelist inclined toward that side. He practiced with us a kind of indulgence based on contempt (if contempt is conceivable in a religious man of that stamp).

I had perceived in him as in so many of the clergy a frustrated man of letters, and hampered by that frustration. I would hesitate to say what the pages he published in *Vigile* were worth. One day when I felt it was the polite thing to praise an article he had written on St. Augustine, he cut in sharply and declared bluntly that he did not concede me the right to judge or even to approve what he wrote.

How and why I finally decided to put a distance between us, whether it was after a misunderstanding I don't know, and would have a hard time clearing up after more than thirty years. Apparently I tried to forget what made the cup overflow, and have succeeded. I was certainly at fault in fleeing without asking for an explanation or even attempting to give one. Today, now that he *has* returned to his Father, I render him justice and attest to the fact that what I owe him infinitely outweighs the faults he may have had, which were due to his dedicated character and the authority it implied in a nature as intractable as his.

At that moment in my life when I was lying in the ditch beside the road, losing blood, he had taken me on his back and carried me to the Inn. Not content with merely handing me over to the care of the inn-keeper, he remained beside me, constantly, unflaggingly, and then he took me to the Benedictine abbey at Solesmes. After that, he came to visit me at Malagar, and accompanied me on a pilgrimage to Lourdes. It was as though I were his only penitent; he had abandoned the ninety and nine other sheep. During this period, his kindness had been without a flaw, although he was scandalized at my bourgeois habits of comfort. Always traveling first class in trains! Always stopping at the best hotel, even at Lourdes! And always at table the foods I preferred—as if I had no reason to do penance, while he was certainly well placed to know the reasons I had to be put on a diet of dry bread and water. But he knew how to be gentle, at those times.

And I believe that, in those days when I judged him severely, I did recall how this good Samaritan had also been a scalp-hunter and found a human satisfaction in his hunt for souls to save. His converts could no longer be counted, but he counted them. I told myself that all the wild game was not of the same weight in his eyes and that I figured in my proper place on a certain fowling list.

Even so, when I parted from Father X, I had just received a blow that changed the color of my life. A gong had sounded in my ears. Death, which cannot be looked at face to face, had extended over me the shadow of a hand quite close but as if still hesitant.

I had barely passed "the midmost of life's journey." I was strong as an oak. From the return to the Christian fountainheads, the writer had drawn benefits. My career as a writer seems always to have profited from everything, even from the Grace of God. No thought overwhelms me more than this. I climbed to the zenith of literature, more decked out than a Montgolfier balloon. Everything went well for me on the two rosters, eternity and time. I had just published *Le Noeud de Vipères*, which had been praised to the skies. The dome of the *Institut* began to emerge from the mist beneath my prudent gaze. And then, one day in 1932 . . .

My health had also improved. I no longer kept late hours. I no longer drank (not that I was ever a great drinker, but at the epoch of the Boeuf sur le Toît the least cocktail acted on my nerves, my liver, and also my morals). Suddenly I lost my voice, and was sent to Combloux for treatment. I returned much fortified, but still voiceless. What followed I shall not tell, although that clap of thunder in a sky as serene as mine made a break in my life and created another sky and another earth.

All is Grace, but that terrible kind of Grace is a two-edged blade. There is nothing to which I am less able to adapt myself than illnesses. And I am astounded that I went through this trial without uttering a cry. Briefly, this is what happened. One afternoon I went to consult a laryngologist to correct a hoarseness on the eve of a lecture I was to deliver at the *Annales*. The doctor examined and reexamined that throat. Finally he declared he wanted to have a consultation with a colleague, a former professor under whom he had studied. And at once he telephoned for an appointment. The other doctor's office was next door and we went immediately, he accompanying me, as if no time could be lost.

I still shudder when I recall that first meeting with Professor Hautant. Later on, for he surrounded me until his death with kindness and unflagging generosity, he confessed that he had, on that dreadful day, dealt me the blow a rescuer administers to prevent a drowning person from struggling. He had to persuade me to enter the clinic next day, and I heard him coldly inform me that I had "eighty chances out of a hundred to be pulled out of this," that my condition had "reached the limit . . ." Yes. At one moment we are standing in the gentle spring sunlight, full of life and strength. The street makes its familiar uproar. My wife is expecting me at home. And then, the next minute . . .

I lack the courage to set foot again in the dark tunnel of the two years that followed. Some diseases are not easily outwitted. Nor am I easily outwitted, since everything turned out as Professor Hautant had given me to hope they would, and I believed him, while at the same time not believing him. When, six months later, he made the trip to Malagar (after having been in a serious road accident which kept us apart for several weeks), he needed to take but one look into my throat to let out the joyful cry: "This time, I've got you!" I believed him and did not believe him.

But I do not intend to render an account of that period of anxiety, nor of all that happened subsequently and the lightning speed of my progress toward the Academy and my election, which was largely due to the menace hovering over me. I learned about this a few years later when Henry Bordeaux solicited my vote for Jacques Bainville, whom we knew to be close to death. "You know," he artlessly confessed, "when you were a candidate, I told our confreres, 'We must not let Mauriac go before he becomes one of us!'" Thus, with the persistence with which all my life I profited by everything, even sickness and death, the tunnel of those years opened out for me with my election to the French Academy.

As a matter of fact, it was at the darkest part of that long defile of the dark years that the election took place, because whether rightly or wrongly I then thought I was having a relapse. Beginning the day after my reception under the *Coupole,* and all the attendant ceremonies, I was subjected to an exhausting series of X-ray treatments. And throughout this, I had to parade, to smile for the cameramen, entertain at dinners . . . Here I will cut short this story. These are "inner memoirs" that I am writing. I must set down what happened within me during that period which lasted more than fifteen years, through World War II, the German Occupation, and the Liberation—indeed, until about 1950.

But I will confess, with mingled surprise and shame, that menace which hovered over my life, far from detaching me from the world and bringing me closer to God, took me instead, imperceptibly, back to the condition in which I had been four years earlier, except for the anxiety linked this time with the animal fear of suffering and dying.

All my attention was centered upon my body. No, I am libeling myself. I knew at the time of my operation and during the hard months that followed some hours of grace and union with God. But gradually as I entered convalescence—a doubtful and uneasy convalescence in which I only half believed—I took up again everything that had formerly attracted me. Once more, as I approached my fiftieth year, I became the young man I had been. Music, which was never for me anything but the voice of my most secret passion, reigned over me as never before; music alone soothed me. It was during this epoch that I discovered Mozart. Upon returning from the exhausting X-ray treatments, I did not go into a church to pray, but instead listened to the records that a friend of mine, Louis Clayeux, played for me on his gramophone. The chamber music of Mozart had been until then unknown to me. What a revelation that was! But I was also fond of a Beethoven record: the *Trio à l'Archidac*, with Cortot, Thibault and Casals.

Today it is with difficulty that I can recall that condition of fervor and fever. The astonishing thing is the way that false spring, that winter flowering lasted, and that I was restored to life—what is called life—for no reason other than to have been on the point of losing it, and that I embraced it then, not fugitively, but in a stubborn and prolonged embrace which nothing could break for almost fifteen years, not even the tragic events of those years from 1935 to 1945.

They tossed me about, those years, they swept me along, but not like a foetus: this was also the period when I plunged into the political fray. How hard it is to see clearly into one's own destiny! For the part I took in the battle for men had nothing to do, it seems to me, with that zest for life that I had then, as a man who had only recently been threatened with death and had been under its shadow. No, on the contrary, it was the Christian in me that reacted with violence over the invasion of Ethiopia, the civil war in Spain, and even, in France, over the plot being hatched at the Institut de France, Quai Conti, at the very time I penetrated beneath the cupola, around the candidature of Charles Maurras, and perhaps already around Maréchal Pétain.

The history of that ill-known period of French politics, or rather, the story of my reactions to it, should be written. The publisher of *Ce que je crois* wants me to write it, and I agree that upon rereading all those now forgotten articles of mine that appeared in *Sept* or in *Temps présent,* I see matter for serious reflection on my conduct which, for me at least, offers some interest. But these memoirs I am at present writing are the memoirs of a more hidden individual than the one that should be followed, step by step, during those sinister years. The German Occupation did no more to bring me closer to God than had my illness. It went in the same direction as had the disease, handing me once more over to the world, without, however, making me indifferent to God. All the articles that I find which were written during and after that period, particularly the political articles, witness to the contrary. But I had become again, as in my youth, a creature divided against itself. I was to remain so until the chill of veritable old age set in. Then the soul was to crop out, uniquely alive, miraculously preserved under the thick layer of passions—preserved by what? Faith is the salt that does not lose its savor. We should also speak of that deep current that had its source in my childhood and which traversed all those fateful years, gushing up finally to the surface beneath the sky. It still reflected the shores (I am referring to my *Bloc-Notes*), but received nothing more than reflections.

XIII

The Permanence of the Soul, the Comfort of Prayer

The chill of veritable old age, I said. Quite small things often take on a striking significance. The other day, a Thursday, just before the Academy sat, as I held out my hand to a fellow-member I recalled that I had already shaken hands a moment earlier, and excused myself. But the thing that alerted me to my absent-mindedness was the fleeting look of worry in the other's eyes, which seemed to signify, "Can it be, by chance, that . . . ?"

In this last phase of life, I am not a little provoked over the way people constantly expect the worst of me; they are ready to believe anything and everything, are resigned to it in advance—if some of them do not even hope for the worst, obscurely, with that taste for others' misfortune men do not avow but experience in spite of themselves.

If your hand trembles as it sets down the cup of coffee, this trembling is noted. It would do no good to recall that your youthful hand also trembled at times. People would shake their heads and say to themselves, "Keep on talking, old fellow!" No matter how pious we are, we must always be careful not to kneel down in public unless we have a prop nearby to help us get to our feet again. The old legs that still bravely render their service on the road have lost the splendid power they once had to lift us up with a bound.

All these trifling signs constitute a diffused diagnosis in which we feel as if sadly shrouded. The desire we have to avoid it plays a great part in our humor which has become rather unsociable, and in our liking for solitude which daily resembles more and more a passion. Even the remarks on how well we look make us despondent. The complimenter knows quite well that he is not believed, and the complimented does not pretend to be fooled. People exclaim over how young an old man looks, whereas they would not dream of trying to convince a hunchback that his back is flatter than it seems.

But once the door of our bedroom is shut, we are no longer seen, that is to say, no longer interpreted. And as we are today, we were always. For of this we are certain, we who know ourselves inside and out: we differ in no way, now that we have reached our decline, from that person who had such flashing eyes and a dark lock of hair on his forehead. However, in those bygone years we had a passport enabling us to circulate everywhere as a young presence. Today no one asks to see our papers; it's not worth the trouble; people have only to look at us to see we are a stranger, since we are old—a stranger from another world, full of the memories of a voyage no one wants to hear about. Even the language is different, and especially the movement of life: no matter that an old heart beats no more slowly than a young heart, the profound disaccord lies in an opposition of rhythm. And even if, as sometimes happens, a young person approaches us, the gulf that separates an old life from a young life cannot be crossed; there is no footbridge, except temporary, between that movement and that immobility.

But I repeat what I said: in the room where the old man finds himself alone, where no one sees him except himself and God, he takes a melancholy pleasure in a certitude of which he does not try to convince anyone (besides, there is no one to convince), a certitude this old man has that he has not become someone else. Oh, the permanence of the soul! The identity of oneself with oneself forever and ever! Neither "diminished"—as perhaps that fellow-Academician thought, when greeted once too many times—nor, moreover, "augmented." But of what use is it to talk about the perfection of the soul that is bound to a weakened and disarmed body? The old man, if he is a Christian, knows the worth of the yardstick of his piety. The God with whom he communes resembles that pauper who came to our house in the evening, when I was a child, to ask for the left-overs. God within us is nourished with what are the left-overs of the world: that is the religion of the old man. The unique grandeur is when a young person gives up everything

(129

before he has lost anything. I have often told myself that the most mediocre priest surely, at one moment in his youth, had that grandeur and will be judged by that moment when he abandoned everything.

Neither diminished nor deprived, nor enriched, the old man sees himself as he always was. Let no one talk to him about the achievements of his life—it is incredible how little we retain of all the things that have flooded us during so many years. The happenings are muddled or forgotten . . . But what about ideas? Fifty years of reading: what remains from it? To those who, like André Gide, worry to the very end about keeping up with current happenings and culture, I want to say, "Cannot you see that you are porous and that the old cracked pitcher can retain nothing?" Life will have flooded us without either enriching or impoverishing us. And here we are at the end of the journey what we were at the beginning: the same intact cliff that the sea has covered and now uncovers.

It is this identity of himself with himself that enchants an old man when he is alone in his room. He is forever that man, forever that young man, that youth, that child. Strangers as they seem to one another, they are all equally myself and mingle in me until they cease to have distinct aspects. Except the child. Bergamin said to me the other day that our childhood walks more slowly than we do, so that it catches up with us only in our declining years. Then it keeps step with the old man and holds him by the hand, as if to cross one last street . . . That child with whom I could be as harsh as Sartre is today with the child Jean-Paul in his memoirs, *Les Mots*. But it would be unjust. And the child Sartre surely was not the little monster he goes at tooth and nail. There was in that child neither more nor less than everything that has rendered Sartre dear to many people . . .

This morning I heard a blackbird singing. Gardens have vanished from this Parisian quarter and I hardly know how that bird manages to live. He manages as we do. He adapts himself to what destiny imposes, as we do, as we have always done and will do until the *"consummatum est"* upon which ends all life.

The song of the blackbird in this dark and snowy morning is a song I am listening to "in all times for ever"; he sings in my memory, he belongs simultaneously to the present and the past. I can see only dimly what the tide that beats endlessly in my mind brings from the depths of my life and lays at my feet: forgotten beings, not always famous and illustrious. It is not Barrès, it is not Bourget that I am recalling this morning, nor Marcel Proust nor Raymond Poincaré. It is only the woman who used to sell freshly baked buns in the garden of the Bordeaux *mairie* when I was five years old. She was called Mme Angely, and in my memory she seems to be inseparable from the old guardian with the flourishing beard who had lost an arm at the battle of Magenta.

I believe I have always been trying, throughout my life, to rebuild that first nest, using no matter what material at hand. During World War I, I very soon reconstituted such a nest, in a room of a village house where I was billeted, and later in an isolated hut in open country, using a few books and some fabrics, the protections of my earliest days—less against the enemy, although we were at the front, than against life as it is, life which is itself the enemy.

But we can never really build again that first nest, for its charm lay in a real presence; in the vicinity of my mother all danger was warded off. Strange, for there never was anyone more subject to anxiety than my mother, and I knew this. She was a veritable breeding-ground of worries and apprehensions, sometimes the one, then the other, and I did not share them, they belonged to her. I would see her gloomy and as full of lightning as a thunder storm, yet inexplicably I felt I had nothing to fear from those sudden tempests, which I rather loved. My mother's anxieties must have had to do with trifling things, although there may have been a few serious worries over properties and money, or health, secrets she kept to herself, rarely alluding to them. Besides, there were no doubt some religious scruples over trifles that she would confide to an old Jesuit, Father Rocanière, who alone could pacify her.

I have spent my life trying to secrete the same protective shell, and an adversary would enjoy finding in this the real reason for my religious faith. He would say that obviously my mother represented to me a visible Providence and that as I grew older I gradually substituted for her an invisible Providence which had been the source of her strength and her ability to overcome her anxieties. That faith existing in some people, of which I am one, may be inherited, a legacy that cannot be refused, although I have known many Christians who, like Jacques Maritain, became so in spite of having been brought up outside any faith. In my case, faith was a portion of an inherited treasure, or rather, my faith is all that remains of that treasure, the rest having been scattered and squandered, annihilated along with my mother whom I so often saw kneeling on her prayer-stool, her face hidden in both her hands.

Why have these thoughts come to me? Because I heard, this morning, the last blackbird in our neighborhood singing. And yet I do not recall that there was ever a blackbird in our stony and almost treeless Bordeaux, except those in the garden of the *mairie* and the Place Pey-Berland. I recall only the crazy shrieks of the blue martins on summer evenings when we stood on the balcony of the school, the day after the distribution of the end of term prizes, waiting for that moment of absolute bliss when the arrival of the railway station bus would be hailed with our loud shouts: "There it is!" A herculean man by the name of Ernest would carry all our bags on his broad back . . . But of what importance is that Ernest? Well, for whom do you think I am writing these things, if not for myself and those who have followed me to these last lines? And if they have followed me, it is because they like to hear me muttering to myself. Old people who no longer have anyone left with whom to talk are prone to talk to themselves.

These days in the depths of winter that herald the spring long before it arrives astound us not so much by their mildness as by a certain quality of light; the sun is trying to delude us. There will be not one bud the more (at least, not at first glance) when, a month from now, my footsteps will awaken the chilled house, still half asleep because the shutters have not been opened on the north side. But the black branches will not be drowned in a clarity more suave than the amazing transparency of this winter morning.

We are still as extraordinarily sensitive to the moods of the seasons as we would be at the unexpected smile of a beloved mistress, usually ill-humored, who has spent her life in deceiving us. And that smile will suffice; we will take her back and expect her to bring us happiness. What happiness? The source was within us, yet it remained bound to the earth, to the shifting sunlight and shadow, to the movement of bare branches, to the song of birds—at least, this was true for us children born and bred in a certain province, in harmony with a countryside that I believed could alone console me when I returned to it at the age of twenty, heavy hearted, as one always is at twenty.

It was a hope almost always deceived. The adorable spring-time was never adorable except in our minds, thanks to the alchemy of memory and what it manages to do with certain moments. But no deception could overcome that hope we children had, children of a certain breed, a certain family of mankind; Maurice de Guérin belonged to that breed, for he returned to his home at Cayla by exhausting rapid stages, as if he hoped to outstrip death and arrive home before it overtook him. It was a consubstantial hope, with us; we felt sure that the return to our birthplace would be enough to cure every wound, provided that the season resembled a certain image we had treasured. But how many times did we complain, "Spring didn't come up to the mark this year . . ." As a matter of fact, even when spring was perfect and adorable, it harmonized, for the adolescent, with a happiness that was inaccessible, never to be reached; spring was a marvelous festival in the midst of which that boy wandered alone and without having been invited. Autumn was the only season that never disappointed him; it brought to all sorrow the necessary accompaniment, the required lighting . . . Thus the seasons were for the belated young romantics that we were.

But the strange thing is that great age has not dispelled that charm, and as I write this I cannot help but imagine what it will be like a month from now, our arrival at twilight, with the contours of the hills wavering through the leafless branches of the hornbeam tree. I do not tell myself that it will perhaps rain on the stakes in the vineyard, the barbed wire, the gnarled black vine-shoots, that the sky will be overcast, and will dull the light which alone transfigures a landscape which after all is commonplace enough.

And then, from the very first minute, the door barely pushed open, I will lose my brother once more, he will die a second time. In that group of the dead waiting for me on the terrace (the farthest rank is now almost invisible), there will be another shade, that of my brother Pierre. Not that he often came to Malagar. Since he was free only in the evenings (when his work at the Bordeaux Medical School left him free), I was afraid of tiring him by urging him to travel those fifty kilometers at night. I hesitated to call him to announce my return. Now that he is no longer here, I have learned that he impatiently waited for that call, waited and hoped. But he, too, was afraid of being a nuisance.

Strange shyness between brothers! It may have been due to the political differences that separated us; we hesitated to remind each other of saddening or irritating incidents. How often we fail to benefit from interchanges with others like ourselves! For instance, since my mother passed away, I feel her presence constantly, and when she was alive I did not doubt that I was doing all I could for her, in those last years when she had become a dull old woman, tormenting and tormented, in giving her a month of my summer holidays. I did not want to live with her and I let it be known; had I been forced to live with her I would have complied, but not without some complaint. Were she to return now, as she sometimes returns at night in my dreams, I would once more be the child sitting on a stool close to her skirts, and it seems to me the day would be too short, that I could never exhaust the mere pleasure of looking at her.

The last time I saw her, in the rue Rolland, Bordeaux, I was leaving on a trip to Spain with Ramon Fernandez. She was worried about that journey by car. I can still see her as she leaned over the banister, watching me go downstairs. And I did not dream of pausing on a step to look up at her once more.

That was a rather insane trip. Although, God knows, we did amuse ourselves in that Madrid of the last months of the monarchy. Upon our return, I counted on stopping briefly to give mamma a kiss, since we were going through Bordeaux. But Ramon was in a hurry to reach Paris. And after all, I thought, I would be seeing my mother at Malagar in a few weeks . . . The obscure shame I felt should have warned me. I kept repeating to myself, "We'll see each other soon, at leisure; what good would it do to stop for a moment to say goodbye?" Yes, it would have been only a moment, but that moment I did not spend with her endures in me, along with some others, and weighs heavily.

Nor did I at all benefit as I should by that last brother who remained on earth. How many times I told myself, "I must remember to ask Pierre . . ." Oh, it was not in regard to anything important. Merely, I wondered if he recalled the treasure we had hidden, for which we had invented a name no one else knew? They were stones we had collected in the Pyrenees, and also some moss-agates—and something else, but what? Maybe he would remember. Did he remember, as I did, an evening in Paris when we walked round and round the Madeleine, endlessly, sharing a certain grief he had, as we had shared in our childhood a slice of that good black bread the tenant-farmers baked? This year, when I enter the salon, where no doubt there will be a bouquet of jonquils, my first glance will be toward the fireplace where he stood leaning against the mantel that last evening.

I do not lament that winter lingers on, this year. It is cold, but I am glad that spring remains ahead of me, intact. Those few mild days at the end of February, which caused the last blackbird in Auteuil to burst into song, do not count, for spring had not yet begun, and I do not enjoy it in peace except at this twilight hour in Malagar. Spring has not yet come, but it is at the door; we have a presentiment of it, cold as the weather is, because spring is primarily the quality of the light, this pale, naked light.

A little earlier each morning I note this sign which Marcel Proust taught me to love, "the raised finger of the day" between the curtains not quite drawn across the window. I do not have to consult my watch; I know the time almost to the minute. And what do I do then? Well, I sometimes recite a few Latin prayers I learned by heart in my childhood: the *Angelus*, the *Veni Sancte Spiritus*, the *Gloria* of the Mass, the *Magnificat*, if I am contented (which is not every day); the *De Profundis* if death is in my soul (as it sometimes is). And why all this Latin at this particular hour rather than at another? Because, as I emerge from sleep, my mind is too sluggish to invent words to converse with the Father as a son should. And so this son relies on the ancient orisons, installing himself in them as a courtier used to install himself in one of the gala carriages which took him where the king wished, without his needing to think about it.

We recited those prayers throughout our childhood, without understanding what they meant. That *Veni Sancte Spiritus*, in which we asked God, before each class, to awake in us the fire of His love, who among us, during those ten years of schooling, ever stopped to think about what that love was and what that fire? The schoolmaster hurried through those sublime verses, muttering them as if ashamed to be condemned to recite those formulas.

Nothing of them is lost, however, and each morning I climb again into the ancient carriages of the court, the same ones into which we children piled at the beginning and end of every class, when the verses rolled along without holding our attention. The old man settles into the old carriage of the coach-houses of his childhood, he looks out, he remembers, his heart melts at the words: "*Sub tuum praesidium confugimus sancta Dei genetrix.*" O Holy Virgin, what has become of the springtimes of yester-year? Their *Angelus* rings in me. But it is not the odor of the springtime that blows through the verses of the *Angelus,* it is the horribly sickening smells of the refectory, smells I liked, all the same, because they were the odors of an hour spent away from the classroom, far from the blackboard, protected from the questions barked at us by a hostile schoolmaster who humiliated me and unleashed the complacent laughter of the class.

In the refectory I did not listen to the lector: "Memoirs of General Marbot, continued . . ." There was enough of that book to last for years, and I am not sure that I ever heard the end of it. I watched the boarding-school pupils stuffing themselves with the food I despised. I pursed my lips, thinking with anticipation of the evening meal at home, almost always succulent. "Oh yes?" you say. "That's what the *Angelus* represents to you? Then you've no reason to boast . . ."

How true! But the *Magnificat* . . . When I climb into that four-wheeled carriage, I find myself on other roads. This is because every one of its verses, even in my childhood, overflowed with an exultation I really felt. We sang the *Magnificat* as we marched into the chapel, in ranks, on the day of our First Communion, between the double row of fond relatives, in the perfume of lilacs, all of us with heads shorn and scrubbed, body and soul alike polished clean as if with pumice stone. It had needed but one night to dispel the torturing scruples of the public confession and arrange for us this entrance in glory into paradise—such, we are told, was our First Communion, "the most beautiful day of our life."

The priest invited us to go ask our parents to forgive us all our past faults and all the unhappiness that we would cause them during our life. Each of us left his place in the ranks, to seek out his family. Those who had lost their mother or father had the right to a supplementary ration of tears. Were I Jean-Paul Sartre, I can imagine what all this would become and the horrible picture I would draw, here, of that sobbing little boy.

As I knelt at the edge of the path, a hand was laid on my shorn head. It was my grandmother, who was waiting her turn to take communion. That hand is still on me after sixty-eight years. Some children were singing the canticle of Gounod: *"Jusqu'à moi vous osez descendre, humilité de mon Sauveur!"* Shall I repeat what Barrès once wrote (and in regard to me, precisely)? Yes: "Even so, these excesses of sensibility make us shudder . . ." But how many of us were there who felt these things as keenly as I did?

And now I am drawing out as much as possible the portion of a certain tearful comedy perfected by specialists who know all the stage tricks; however, what remains is what the verses of the *Magnificat* continue to spill over for the old man that child of 1896 has become. Criminal life has relentlessly tried to vanquish that joy, but without succeeding. *"Et exultavit spiritus meus . . ."*

The Latin prayers of the morning have lured me far from my subject, which had to do with this springtime that I enjoy only when it has not yet begun; for scarcely shall I enter into it than I shall feel it stricken, fatally wounded, and it will no longer be there. Never was a cliché closer to reality than the one that has always confounded the youth of man with the spring of the year: no sooner are they born than they dissolve. They exist only in what must be called a state of undoing.

The myth of youth resides in this idea of it as a stable state, an established power that we flatter and celebrate. But no sooner have we finished burning our incense than, already, a different visage appears through the smoke, and we do not recognize it. If we write for one generation, the one that reads the article or book we destined for it has become another and its watchwords have changed.

Surely there never was a spring as putrid and mud-soaked as this one; if so, I do not recall it. Anyway, the springs we recall are memorable, not because of their rain or shine, but because of circumstances in our lives, a joy or a grief they brought us with their fogs or showers. But it has now been many years since spring brought me any emotion when it is deprived of sunlight, not even sadness. From now on I live beyond that melancholy of former times, which was really only another kind of delectation.

I should therefore be less reluctant than in my youth to enter, at this season of the year, the Pascalian Mystery and, without noting the color of the sky, should find it easier to revive in spirit that very dolorous story commented on in the liturgy. But such is not the case, and I was never so ill prepared as I am today. Perhaps it is because these thoughts have become familiar, for I set them going every day; at every Mass I attend I am invited to partake of the Last Supper, in that fraction of bread. The Lamb of God is offered up to His Father beneath our eyes: each time we take communion it is Holy Thursday.

Also, the renewal of the liturgy today creates an atmosphere in the holy days very different from that which surrounded them in my childhood. I do not recognize any feature that I loved so ardently in that epoch when we crowded around the temporary altars and when we ran from parish to parish as if for a pious carnival. I feel obscurely disconcerted and disappointed, whereas I should rejoice. Shall I never rid myself of this sentimentality which fools devout Catholics of my stamp into believing that we are Christians when perhaps there is not one ounce of veritable piety in us, not even a grain of a mustard-seed of faith?

Besides, it is an exaggeration to declare that I am in no way helped by the Church ceremonies, especially in the country. The sacraments are what help me, not what precedes and follows them. And while, quite rightly, the Church today attaches so much importance to the life of the community, and while such a great effort is made to promote it in so many parishes, nothing inclines me to it, and I can never have enough silence or solitude for my efforts at prayer. I am almost always disturbed by the presence of others, even when I try to feel at one with them. There prevails, especially in the country churches, such inconsonance between the ritual gestures, chant, words, and the mystery which is being accomplished, that I am overcome.

Perhaps a moment arrives in the life of every Christian when nothing any longer subsists but the remission of sins and the reality of the Living Bread. This reality runs through the impeccable liturgy of Solesmes, neither better nor worse than at a frightful altar lit by electric lamps in a dusty and deserted provincial chapel.

Whether there is a crowd of people or only a few prostrate women in an empty nave, there is always the multiplication of the loaves of bread, that miracle which has continued uninterrupted since the first Holy Thursday. In a world where it is generally understood by so many men that God is dead, that there is no God, that no longer can this be even argued, the breaking of the Eucharistic bread has become more frequent, more worldwide, more usual than in the so-called periods of faith. The Church needed only to relax the rules of sacramental fasting, increase the number of late Masses and evening Masses to bring about a renewal of the Holy Thursday each day in many lives which are sustained only thanks to that daily fraction of bread.

What an incomprehensible mystery, I reflect, every time (and again this morning) I read some article glorifying surrealism, what a mystery that a whole generation has been attracted by those dark shadows, by that mechanical absurdity, that black madness, while there happened in the world almost two thousand years ago an event also in a certain way magical, surpassing all other wizardries—an event that constitutes a unique case, and which still continues. It endures, it witnesses its efficacity in millions of lives. Something occurs everywhere in the world at the same hour. And what occurs is what took place almost two thousand years ago, on a Thursday night extending into the dawn of a certain Friday.

Christianity is not a philosophy, is not a system of thought, it is no other than a story of something that happened, a "really true story" as children say, and it still endures. Humanity is quite like that child we were who did not mind at all hearing the same story told over and over. And the better he knew the story the more he loved it. And we too, we know the Passion by heart, but we know it less from the recital of it than through the experience we have of it and shall have had perhaps ever since the first betrayal by the Judas kiss until the hour that will be our hour to stretch out on a certain cross that has been kept for us, and commit our soul to God.

A magical story, if ever there was one, yet which is true and is verified by its efficacity, as we are all witness, we who live it. And how can it horrify those who have nonetheless a passion for the *"surréal"* and should be attracted by the supernatural? Thus everything is taking place according to what Christ Himself said to Nicodemus: ". . . men loved darkness rather than light, because their deeds were evil."*

No other truth but that one has been given to man; but it is an unendurable mystery that the surrealists overlook, they who should have been the best qualified to understand and adore it. As for those who repudiate and most deliberately hate it, their hate and their repudiation seem to be commensurate with the possibilities they initially had to walk in the light . . .

---

* John 3:19

Epilogue: *Nunc dimittis*
servum tuum Domine

These musings and reflections should end here, on the tip of the promontory where they have set down the living old man. Yes, his *Bloc-Notes* testify to the fact that he is still alive, for apparently he is still interested in politics. Indeed, his main interest became politics in recent years, and the same inclination that has attached him to current history has detached him from fiction, from the novels he might have written, like those that others have been writing. This should be enough to show how and why the political man in me is linked with the Christian: I would never have been so preoccupied with eternal matters had I not become involved in timely affairs.

Now I must ask myself one last question: Tell me, what do you think of yourself? What has this long contemplation of your destiny awakened in you? I concede that it was a guarded contemplation; I have seen only what I wanted to see. These pages, therefore, do not contain my whole life; the reader can invent or find the missing pieces that are needed to complete the jigsaw puzzle. I am not at all worried. Gradually, as I approach the farthest boundary, I am enclosed in the silence that cloaks a tomb, no matter how illustrious. You would say that the human mind, saturated with memories, renounces remembering anything more. This thought is both overwhelming and reassuring. The survivors, to justify the oblivion that engulfs the great dead, dispute their title to greatness. Once the man has disappeared, there remains his *oeuvre*—and often not even that (Proust, Claudel, Valéry excepted).

I have no illusions or qualms, aside from the regret over not leaving behind me an indisputable monument. What strikes me, rather, when I consider my life, is the disproportion between the means I initially disposed of and the result I obtained. My winnings seem enormous to me when I consider the paltry wager. That little

(141

provincial from a bourgeois family, alien to real culture, educated in a lycée where the intellectual level was hardly one to elevate the mind, that student bereft of mathematics, little gifted in philosophy, ignorant of foreign languages and therefore dependent upon translations, became, even so, a member of the Academy very early in life, obtained an honorary doctorate at Oxford, was awarded the Nobel Prize in Literature. That sedentary who fears the airplane, who hates any other mode of travel than what he accomplishes by motor-car twice a year, between the Avenue Théophile Gautier in Paris and Malagar château near Bordeaux, and who no doubt will die without ever having seen New York, and without having seen almost anything of the world (and recalling very little of what he has seen), that slippered stay-at-home managed to become a well-known journalist, admired by his adversaries—so well-known that he arouses jealousy on the part of the novelist he thinks he is. That bourgeois who instinctively detests risk will nonetheless have run a great many big risks, brandishing his pen with a greater boldness than many of his peers would ever have been capable of doing.

Thus there was in me, beneath an apparent weakness and perhaps springing from it, a hidden force which will continue to exert itself to my final hour. One word expresses it: I am a poet. Why should I care that others have refused to acknowlege this? For I know I am a poet and have never been anything else; I suppose my inability to be recognized as a poet makes me to that extent a failure—or rather I would have been, had not an imperceptible well of poetry fed everything I have written, whether fiction, essays, or the most trifling magazine article.

What I would not be able to enlarge upon here, for the subject would exceed the bounds of these memoirs, is the fact that the hidden well of poetry I mention is, in its turn, nourished by an even more hidden spring: the Grace of God. The two sources of inspiration, that of the earth and that of God, will have produced this troubled flood.

And this flood has borne me up. But it is usual to mention, when one has summed up one's life, what one has done for self-advancement. On this point, the more I think about it the more I believe that my bourgeois and countryman heritage played a part. My success was not due to calculations, to Balzacian plans. The rather artless lad of 1910 may have dreamed of imitating Rastignac or Rubempré, but that simpleton would not have gone very far. Truly, the elements that were useful to my literary career were not the product of deliberate schemes. From my bourgeois family of merchants and landed gentry, I learned that order was the essential virtue and the primordial duty was to avoid all risk. Thus, from my birth onward, I was instinctively on guard against everything tending to dilapidate the patrimony or damage reputation or health. Instinct alone functioned. This lack of a calculated plan, and the fact that I never thought about it, made me, precisely, avoid all the wire-pulling that the Nobel jury detests; those who never think about it are often the ones who carry off the prize.

I neither praise nor blame myself: I was that poet, and I was that bourgeois maneuvered at long distance—one might say "tele-guided"—by my forebears, and I was that Christian, too.

That Christian. I had something to give. And it is through this that I shall have counted for something, no matter how little. I had something to give, a not very common attribute of writers, except in the artistic sense, for everyone worthy of the name of artist has something to give in that respect. I had a message to convey—not that I was alone in this, but many others who could have assumed the responsibility, as I did, had shunned or forgotten it. I carried on. I do not boast of this, for this morsel of bread remained at the bottom of my mendicant's bag mingled with many scraps, the miserable objects of my cupidities. Almost unwittingly, I was to distribute that bread, at certain periods in my life. A turbid novel such as *Destins* marked the beginning of a very religious calling, and it bore rich fruits. Such and such a Carmelite nun would perhaps not be a Carmelite nun today had not *Thérèse Desqueyroux* been written. Strange but true, for no one could be more unworthy of his vocation that I was of mine, but I had to say what I had to say, could not avoid it.

Such was my chance, my good fortune. And if you ask me, "Were you, then, happy?" I would reply that yes, I had that blessing. Success, what is called success and which is always so relative, is not happiness but is a life-belt that keeps the exhausted swimmer afloat. Such gratifications have nothing to do with our real and boundless hunger and thirst which will need all eternity to be appeased.

I have had no other happiness in the world except to believe in this calling, nor other unhappiness except over having been so faint-hearted in complying with it, in failing to conform my life to it, while never abdicating. Was I looking for an alibi to cheat God? Did I waste my vocation in worldly actions and passions? I have never known whom I was trying to fool, whether it was God or society or myself that I betrayed.

There had to be this self-examination in the last hour of twilight for me to amend my ways. Until the very threshold of old age and well beyond it, I struggled against inhibitions blindly, not wanting to know what they signified.

It sometimes happens that I succumb to regrets and feel a miserable nostalgia when I think of all the things I have missed in life. And yet, I know that human love is often misplaced. There is in all love an ineffable moment or moments, a meeting point, a miraculous coincidence, but in a day and sometimes in an hour the one and the other go separate ways, and if the liaison endures, this in no way alters the fact; theirs is a double solitude, they are bound together in twin solitudes.

Physical love is not the love of human beings. To possess and enjoy the body of another to the point of satiety, of disgust, is not the worst of it; indifference is worse, and it even overcomes resentment. That the obsession turns into boredom, whether slowly or rapidly, is the fate of passionate love and makes marriage what we nearly always see it is. We consider a certain face, we listen to a certain voice, and we try to recall the time when that face darkened or lit up the world for us, when the air we breathed was less essential to our life than that thrilling voice. For now it has become a face like any other, a voice like any other; perhaps not quite, for a very faint trace is always left of an old scar.

And if I am here calumniating passionate love, I ask forgiveness of the couple, if such exists, in which both partners, throughout their lives, have loved each other with what is called love, and have known here on earth that eternal moment, and have not succumbed in that defeat represented by love that has become friendship, passion transformed into tenderness. Veritable love does not change. It is, or it never has been.

I sometimes toy with the idea that this exactingness in human beings who are made to love and have never known anything but to love, may have been strong enough to invent an object of love commensurate with its demands. Was it perhaps this compelling need of the human heart and its incoercible passion that created God? This would refute Lucretius who taught that fear created the gods. If, according to you—I am now addressing myself to unbelievers—man issued from matter and is nothing else and will return to matter, if, even so, man has been capable of inventing God and a God in no way an idol of wood, metal, or stone, not a sensual and libidinous idol, but one drawn from all the sweetness and strength in mankind, all his power and weakness, in short, love and its infinite demands, then what a marvel that would be! And still more marvelous would be a God so invented and endowed with utterances which after almost two thousand years continue to be the spirit and life of the world . . . No. Such a thing is impossible and can only appear possible to those who have not experienced Christianity intensely but know it only from historical criticism and the study of comparative religions and myths.

In sum, this sacramental life is a part of my daily joys. If my faith were but the size of "a grain of mustard-seed" should I fear death, or would I not on the contrary desire it? Have not all the saints desired it? This is a reproach that is never made to us who are the worshippers of the God close to the human heart, and hence a source of joy, of the most human of joys.

Christian sweetness penetrates the destiny that these memoirs reflect—but like all other sweetness, like the fondled childhood, like the tenderness of my mother, like the sleep I sank into in the bark moored to her bed, in the depths of the bedroom where the shadows moved as the fire flickered out; and I heard a boat siren in the port, the whistle of a locomotive, the wheels of a late fiacre.

I can poorly distinguish eternity from the transience of time. I am afraid of having confounded what is God with this part of my being, the most attached to the ephemeral and to all that is past and gone. On the day of my death, however, I will not bid farewell to God! I will not leave Him as I will leave all the rest, since I will go toward Him. This I know, but I do not feel it. I ought to mistrust my liking for those prayers my mother recited aloud and which no one in the world knows today; and for the forgotten canticles of my childhood, those especially of my First Communion: such tastes are the sign that I have taken aboard the Infinite Being and the Incarnate Word along with everything that has nourished my dreams and served to delight me; these and the rest of the cargo are taken aboard.

I ought to end on this doubt, this anxiety which will never leave me: I wonder if one ounce of authentic Christianity is to be found in these pages which seem to overflow with it. What else can I do? I have been that man and no other. And yet what I show of him here is only the best and most affecting of his characteristics . . .

No, I have told enough, perhaps too much. Besides, what does it matter! When I am gone, what will remain of these pages? There will remain what remains of the buzzing of those fields in the late afternoons of bygone summer holidays, the rustling of the leaves when the moon ruled the sky, and when I stood motionless and barefoot on the wooden balcony that was still warm from the day's sunshine, when I was fifteen years old.

Not one ounce of authentic Christianity, did I say?

Here in my study at Malagar, the eyes of that man portrayed by Michel Ciry gaze steadily down at me, and I do not know if his eyes express condemnation or pardon. For that man is the Christ—I know this, although Ciry's sketch in no way resembles the Son of God as traditionally depicted by painters and sculptors down the centuries. This drawing that hangs on my study wall looks more like the glorious Christ of Byzantium and the Sindon of Turino. He is frail, his unkempt hair straggles down over the forehead in a way that reminds me of Charles Péguy. His hollow cheeks, covered with a thin beard, have been buffeted and spat upon. The eyes of that pitiful man are focused on me here in my modest study, where everything has been done to provide me with privacy, repose, and isolation. I wanted to feel cut off, separated from my fellow-men, and that is what this study signifies.

I look questioningly at that condemned man, mortally sad, who resembles no one else; Michel Ciry perhaps made that sketch without knowing that Christ would manifest Himself in it, and in a particular form, not, I believe, as my judge, but as an examiner wanting to make me overwhelmingly aware of the contradiction in my life.

It is upon that contradiction that I want to arrest my attention for the last time. In the final pages of these memoirs I must, through this meditation, put the final touches on the image of myself and of my life which I have here embellished, presenting myself in a way calculated to disarm my readers rather than to enlighten them.

So I will now substitute the old man of letters as seen by the Lord from the depths of His agony. On which one of my weaknesses does He pass judgment, if He is judging me? And if He does not judge me, what is it in me that renders Him so melancholy? Have I ever known? Would I not have become aware, during these last days of my life on the threshold of death, without anyone to intervene for me with that Man who is gazing down at me?

From my youth onward I have claimed the name of Christian and from the time when I began to write I have gloried in the name. I wrote as if my mission were to proclaim the Christ. And from the beginning I believed that this, at least, would be counted for me at the Last Judgment and that the Lord would keep His promise to all those who had confessed Him before mankind and would, in His turn, not deny us before His heavenly Father. I felt reassured.

But that Lamb of God now gazing down at me would not be sad as only a God can be sad, if I had reason to be reassured and comforted. There are some who have left Him, who have seemed to deny Him, while I have apparently remained faithful; I will admit that those others have been more consistent, because they did not think it was possible to gamble on Christ and on the world, simultaneously, as I have done.

Such is the contradiction in my life. It is too blatant to be dissimulated. It is fundamental, and I doubt whether the denial of those who have not consented to serve both God and Mammon and have chosen Mammon is worse than the compromise to which I resorted.

Those eyes of God resting on me are taking the exact measure of a man of letters. And to begin with, He sees all that part of me which was imposed upon me from birth. Recently I have been reading a doctoral thesis called "Mauriac or fidelity to sensation," which has certainly not taught me anything about myself. Still, after reading it, I understood better to what point I was, from childhood on, molded or rather recreated by that narrow world in which I was born and became what I am, taking from that hive enough honey to nourish me and my *oeuvre* all my life.

From the very first steps I took, the die was cast. I could be no other than that bourgeois offspring who, thanks to poetry, would transfigure that heritage of merchants and landowners . . . But the substance of that transfiguration was comprised of farms and vine-yards, with their population of tenant-farmers, servants, and stewards. It was a small, self-contained universe, enclosing a fixed idea of a quiet and studious life sheltered from all risk and all human contact—aside from the contact with those who would provide some advantages and amenities, a chance of happiness, or at least a promise of pleasure.

I could not have been any other than that bourgeois child. Yes, I could have dominated it, could have opposed to such a paltry delectation "the victorious delectation of Grace." I could have become another, like all the saints, for sainthood is that reversal of the whole being which made of the heroic missionary, Father de Foucauld, a person without a single feature in common with the person who had been, that young and almost portly army officer, Lieutenant Comte Charles de Foucauld. But then my crime would be to have been myself instead of trying to throttle the man that inevitably sprang from the infant I had been, an infant formed and trained by a pious mother and monkish schoolmasters, but also and to a greater degree by those inherited estates, forests, and vineyards with all they imply in preconceived ideas on the need for each social class to keep its place, and on the privileges sanctioned by the rents from the tenant-farmers. We bourgeois children could no more be blamed for having been born in a comfortable or even opulent environment than "the little paupers" (as one said at that time) deserved praise for having been born in a hovel.

No, no, this cannot be the cause of the pity I seem to see in those eyes gazing at me with God-like attention; those eyes may see in me, relatively speaking (though we cannot be compared), what I see in Him. And what could that be? What do we have in common? The cross. This insignificant bourgeois, like all human beings, was also crucified. He was not always aware of it, was not conscious of it every minute of his life. But now that everything is consummated he clearly sees that he too was crucified, neither more nor less than any other. Everyone is crucified, even the ones apparently the most fortunate. We are not presumptuous in believing this. We do not glorify ourselves for sharing the common lot, we neither desired nor chose it, and have unceasingly wanted to descend, and in fact have descended from the cross. But we remain bound to the cross, no matter how far we have tried to flee it. And He who looks down on us knows that all this mediocre luxury, all this comfort, all the brilliance of a successful career combine to constitute the armature of a suffering in no way singular, for it is the most commonly distributed thing in the world. And this explains why there are so many alcoholics and drug addicts: diversion—the *divertissement* analyzed by Pascal—whether innocent or guilty, harmless or polluted, responds to the need to flee or forget that is felt by all men from childhood on.

But I was a Christian. I knew that with the saints tears of joy are shed and that joy was what I knew to be the condition and the price. I neither consented to the one nor desired to pay the other. The strange thing is that, while continuing to lead the routine life of society as I did, I continued to react to everything as an intransigent Christian, not hypocritically, but impelled by my nature, and very strongly impelled, without reflection, as if bound to say and write certain things that I alone could say and write, as if being the man I was, no matter what my life might be, I was still playing the part that had been assigned to me from the very beginning. I have never ceased to be surprised at the number of souls reached and saved through my books, even those considered the most disturbing. How amazing it is that, through me, the one who has given nothing, many others have given all.

I am writing this at Malagar, sheltered within the crumbling walls of the unpretentious manor house. I did not choose this country seat, the house, the wine-making establishment, still standing, although in my infancy my mother thought they were all about to collapse. I did not choose Malagar; I inherited it and adorned it with objects that were for the most part also inherited. And this calls to mind some lines written by André Lafon, addressed to a man who had fallen upon bad times:

"I shall not tell him, 'You should have . . .' nor ask him 'Why?'
Since we play so small a part in fashioning our lives."

(149

We play so small a part in fashioning our lives. I do not repeat this as an excuse, for I feel responsible for my own life. It could have been whatever I wanted it to be and I am forever what it has been. I repeat it as defense against an unmerciful censure. The Grace of God must always have been within reach, and it would have been able to quell temptation, even the constant temptation of a young human animal overflowing with the forces of life. For that Grace has such strength that, even when apparently vanquished, it still acts, utilizing its very defeat: we conform to the cross not only through our sufferings, but through our sins, our backslidings, and this obscure and endless defeat to which all lives come.

It is on this plane, in the deepest, most hidden and personal elements of my life, that I feel, nay, experience Christian verity, and not in its external manifestations, even the most worthy of approbation, not even in the meritorious effort being made in the Church to create a communal life and arouse a fraternity such as that which, on the day after the crucifixion of the Lord, persevered in prayer and in the breaking of the bread. There is always something forced and artificial in any resort to technique. The aspirations of each individual (especially the young) to establish a secure temporal life must always be adapted to his Christian aspirations—which implies a compromise.

The real dialogue is carried on in our inmost self, in the deepest solitude; it is a dialogue which does not tend to create a certain climate or assemble a faithful flock to receive orders, but merely brings our creature self to a confrontation with that God who is now watching me. Nothing is of importance outside that confrontation, for which the Church provides the means with proven efficacity. Two sayings of the Christ are addressed to all, to each individual who consents to hear them. They are: "Your sins are forgiven . . ." and "This is my body . . ." For my part I regret the phrase the Church has recently omitted at the moment of the fractioning of the sacred Host: *"Corpus domini nostri Jesu Christi custodiat animam tuam . . ."* The Dominicans say: *"custodiat te . . ."* which circumscribes still more the tête-à-tête of the communicant and the Lord.

Everything that crystallizes around these two sayings which establish the remission of sins and attest to the real Presence—

superbly crystallizing in the abbeys or in the illustrious old parishes of the great Catholic cities, or poorly and miserably in the almost deserted village churches—counts no more for me, enchants me no more, troubles me no more . . . Or rather, yes! I have often made the confession: there is a stumbling block which perturbs me, that Incarnation, of which so few human beings have become aware, and which has not even become known throughout entire continents. I console myself (I dare not say "reassure myself") only by recalling what the Lord told us about the kingdom of God which is like the morsel of leaven needed to make the dough rise: "a little leaven leaveneth the whole lump."*

We must concede that if the Church seeks the secret of her renewal, it is because the structures of the edifice have aged and appear to be intolerable, less to the congregations than to many of the clergy confined within its antique armature. But I no longer suffer from such fits of impatience, now that I am an old man as burdened with years as was that beggar in my infancy who carried on his back a bag full of crusts and came to stand in the kitchen doorway on certain days. Death is at the door now, and what counts for me is less to change the rusty conduits of Rome than what still flows through them, here and now, from the two sayings in regard to the remission of sins and the consecration of the bread.

But where does this yearning for pardon come from? A feeling of guilt so out of proportion with what my life was, is it inscribed in the nature of every child born into this world (the moral law within us, according to Kant, attests the existence of God), or is it a deformation occurring in infancy, imposed upon the Christians of my kind, and which I have not known how to cure? These bands, these bonds that have been broken by Anglo-Saxon Puritans, German Lutherans, Latin Catholics, and so many writers and philosophers, broken as soon as they began to think, will continue to bind me tightly to the very end. I acknowledge it and am troubled by the fact at times. But then what I observe of those presumably liberated men reassures me: it is of no use to decide that evil is good, as almost all of them do.

This determined goal of happiness felt by human beings, this

---

* 1 Cor. 5:6

refusal to see what is blindingly obvious, that we must die, which comes down to saying that no matter how old one lives to be, one must die, well, there is nothing more strange or absurd—yet in a way nothing more admirable. Everything man erects between himself and death, all these structures which testify for centuries to the creature he really is, entitled to God and, in a certain amount, participating in God, surely this is admirable.

Evil exists, I know from my own experience, and because I know mankind; therefore, good exists, I have encountered it in the saints and have seen it in those we call "the lambs." And death is there, perhaps close at hand. Whoever does not take into account that trinity of evidence does not interest me, rather, is alien to me; we do not speak the same language.

"They that are whole have no need of the physician, but they that are sick: I came not to call the righteous, but sinners to repentance." * But who is righteous? And sinners, when they know they are sinners, are they not the sole people who may be called righteous? To know oneself to be a sinner, to have that knowledge which is already expiation—this is the fountainhead of all authentic Christian life. There is no other, and bad Christian that I have been, at least this knowledge has assured me of this authenticity.

Is it knowledge acquired or inherent knowledge? This individual that my "memoirs of my inner life" reflect by deforming him, the individual at whom the Christ of Michel Ciry gazes and sees him as he has been, as he is, and will always be, what kind of person would he have been had he lost his mother at birth, instead of his agnostic and perhaps atheistic father? Yes, supposing it had been my agnostic father who took charge of my education rather than that pious young widow, overly scrupulous, held under the not at all light yoke of an old Jesuit confessor?

I have often asked myself this question, ever since I wrote *Commencements d'une vie*, but without seeking the reply and as if it went without saying that such a question can have no reply. As a matter of fact, if I concentrated my mind on this, that is to say, were I to put the question, not to the reader, that invisible person who makes us strike a pose, but to myself and God, if I dared say it, I am

---

* Mark 2:17

not sure that I would find the reply; at least I would end up with some more pressing and immediate questions. Perhaps it would not be impossible to disengage what existed in me before any education, that is, the portion which is consubstantial and whose dark waters have seeped through all the bulwarks. Indeed, what that devout mother imposed upon me was in no way calculated to contain that tide but much rather to make the water level rise and perhaps overflow and flood everything and utterly destroy my faith in God . . . Yes, the more I reflect, the more I believe that the piety learned at my mother's knees was not the conclusive factor—all the less so, when I recall how soon my reading developed a critical mind in me, and the spirit of mockery. This old polemicist that I have become existed powerfully in the child, especially in the adolescent, whom my mother reproved for "finding everyone stupid." Yes, I found everyone stupid, and particularly so in the stifling clerical atmosphere that surrounded me. I saw many who broke away. But mock as I would and pretend to break the bonds that held me, I did not break away and have never believed it would be possible for me to do so.

Certainly the upbringing I had gave to my religious life, quite early, a particular accent, narrowed it, intensified the scruples of a conscience naturally troubled and distressed. However, it would be equally accurate to say that I did not lose my faith, in spite of that education.

A secret force within me overcame the repulsion I felt—not for religion, which I loved in spite of everything, but for the Christians in my immediate circle, Pharisees, enemies of any culture, rejecting the modern world but likewise rejected by that world. The Catholics of today cannot even imagine the storm that was brewing in the Church at the time of St. Pius X, when I was twenty—and it cannot be denied that a certain anxiety fostered by my upbringing would have made me adhere to the faith; I was the child who clung to his mother's hand when crossing a street, and who throughout life never relinquished it. But I do not believe the scoffer in me, existing along with a passionate tenderness leading to attachments and suffering, would have eventually broken the bonds of faith had there not been that Presence within me which manifests itself at this very moment: the countenance of a divine love from which I have received everything, while refusing to give what that love demands of every life it has penetrated.

(153

My formation owed almost nothing to my schooling. As a matter of fact, I was really not a brilliant pupil, I was not intelligent in the sense used when speaking of a *"cagneux"*—which means not only a "skrimshank" but also a pupil preparing for entrance to the prestigious École Normale Supérieure. I never understood any idea that was not one I myself had secreted or discovered. I was unable ever to learn anything from a schoolmaster because I had only a dim understanding of ideas I had not myself formulated. If the worth of a body of work is measured by its singularity and particular characteristics which render it different from all others, it must be closely dependent upon what constituted the nature of its author and his character, the product of a narrowly circumscribed heredity and environment.

It is thus that the "All is Grace" pronouncement of Bernanos and Saint Theresa takes its human significance: everything occurs as if Someone had utilized the elements furnished by a certain heredity and environment to fashion lovingly a certain human being different from others, different from anyone who has existed or will ever exist. All is Grace: which signifies that God utilizes everything, even the mediocre or vulgar, even the worst—especially perhaps the worst, as it appeared in the story of Magdalene, whom the Saviour loved more than the others because He had forgiven her more than the others.

"O ye hypocrites," our Lord exclaimed, "ye can discern the face of the sky; but can ye not discern the signs of the times? A wicked and adulterous generation seeketh after a sign ..." * We who have seen neither sign nor wonder, and who have remained faithful to that Church which is at present casting off the dead skins of old rituals, have fundamentally remained faithful to that Someone; it is to that current of supernal life that we have remained faithful, that trickle of Grace which found its way to us through the scoria of the creed, but that trickle of water has sufficed to keep us from dying of thirst.

"That Church which is at present casting off the dead skins of old rituals ..." I will be accused of having pursued my meditation throughout these Memoirs, as if there were no one in the universe

---

* Matt. 16:3–4

but me and my Creator. And yet I belong to a Church which under the papacy of John XXIII and at this very moment (Paul VI has just returned from his pilgrimage to the Holy Sepulchre) has consoled me from all the blows she dealt me in the past.

To end with, I must give thanks, and must find something of the thrill of joy that inspired the old Simeon with his *"Nunc dimittis servum tuum Domine . . ."* For I, too, in this day of my old age, have seen much that, in my youth, I could not have dared hope to see.

This pilgrimage of the Holy Father to Jerusalem, this return of Simon-Peter to his native land toward the end of the two thousand years of the Christian era has astonished the world, a world that recalls having once been Christian but is no longer sufficiently so to comprehend the true reasons for its astonishment. What, after all, is strange in this pilgrimage of the Pope to Bethlehem, Nazareth, and Jerusalem? Would not the strange thing be, rather, that he was the first of St. Peter's successors, if not to have had the thought, at least to have carried it out? Indeed, something has happened in the Church, an immense event in which this return to the source by the chief of the Apostles will have been but an episode: it manifests to the eyes of the world that the death of Pope John has not interrupted his miraculous papacy. There still breathes the same spirit that breathed upon that old diplomat-prelate—whom I knew well, when he was the papal nuncio in Paris. He was so sensitive, so gentle, and dare I say, so droll? And he gave no hint of grandeur, so that never for a moment did I foresee that he would one day be that inspired man, that revolutionary, that saint; and now the same spirit has taken hold of Paul VI with supernatural and literally divine force. And we have seen the speeding up of history become beneath our very eyes an acceleration of Grace.

This miracle in the Church of 1964 is hard to define. It marks the end of an enchantment. From the sixteenth century on, the Vatican had been immobilized, as if spellbound, as if condemned to an eternal pomp, an incurable ostentation. Its guards with their doublets, helms, and halberds had become the guards of the Sleeping Beauty and had waited for more than four centuries for the gouty hands of an old man to come and wake them up. That splendor to which the popes of the Renaissance had sacrificed close to half of the Christian world (since the basilica of St. Peter was built with the money of those same indulgences which aroused the revolt of Luther), that splendor encircled Holy Church, and the Vatican, isolated in the midst of the world, became literally a prison.

In vain, the Counter-Reformation, the enchanted circle opened no more. The ring of the fisherman had become enlarged to the dimensions of the marvelous palace, and the Pope appeared there in the distance, motionless, crushed under the weight of too many crowns and copes, as if ankylosed with power. Sometimes he was carried on the *sedia gestatoria*, above a sea of humanity. But Simon-Peter could no longer descend from that too heavily gilded bark, nor walk on the sea in the presence of his God and Saviour.

In the enchanted palace, Simon-Peter could do nothing but jealously guard the sacred trust committed to him. He saw to it that not one iota was changed, not one comma misplaced; and among his flock, whether of the laity or the clergy, he was suspicious of any spirit of enquiry.

Outside, however, the world had changed. The world had not waited to return to its pagan sources. The spirit of free enquiry opened the way to the century of Voltaire, then to the century that was to proclaim the death of God. And then, the more the Church entrenched herself from the world, the more inclined was the world of men to shake off all constraint. From 1870 on, the enchanted ring tightened still more round the infallible and fulminating Pope. The bronze doors shut him in—hermetic like the doors of Noah's ark which preserved Noah from the universal havoc.

The idea of indefinite progress had broken down as a result of the two scientific and technical mass slaughters of 1914 and 1939. Nothing, however, allowed us to foresee that the Church of Rome was about to attempt a sortie toward this doomed world.

When the abomination of desolation reached its peak with Hitler, the silence of the Vatican, which still makes some people indignant, was more than ever the silence of a prisoner. Pius XII, on June 2nd, 1943, conceded this before the Sacred College of Cardinals: "The Vicar of Christ," he exclaimed, "who appealed only for pity and a sincere return to the elementary norms of justice and humanity, found himself confronting a door that no key could open."

Epilogue: Nunc dimittis servum tuum Domine

Splendid as was the prison and its walls covered with the frescos of Michelangelo and Raphael, it nonetheless muffled the horrible cries in the outside world. "Whatsoever thou shalt bind on earth shall be bound in heaven," * Christ has promised Peter. And it was himself that Peter had bound, during all the Middle Ages and until the Council of Trent, through his desire for temporal power. And afterwards, in spite of all the mercies that Holy Church showered upon the earth, especially in the time of Pius XI, promoter of native clergies, the sovereign pontiff remained a prisoner, until the advent of Pope John.

Then was renewed the miracle recounted in the Acts of the Apostles, when an angel freed Simon-Peter from the prison where Herod had cast him: "And, behold, the angel of the Lord came upon him, and a light shined in the prison: and he smote Peter on the side, and raised him up, saying, Arise up quickly. And his chains fell off from his hands. And the angel said unto him, Gird thyself, and bind on thy sandals. And so he did. And he saith unto him, Cast thy garment about thee, and follow me." **

Paul VI also binds on his sandals, wraps his cloak about him, and takes to the road. In truth, we are at the beginning of Christian history if, as it is written in an Epistle of Peter: "One day is with the Lord as a thousand years, and a thousand years as one day." *** Everything is but just beginning. The baleful spell cast by the Borgias and the Borgheses has been broken. John XXIII did not even need to push the folding bronze door open; he was already consoling the sick in a hospital and visiting prisoners. The spirit of God engulfed the Vatican when the bronze door was barely half open. And the world received this breath of God like a strong wind, not merely the faithful but even that portion of the human species who proclaim themselves atheists; and the world saw with astonishment that old man standing on the illustrious threshold, and he did not condemn but blessed that part of the human species and raised above them his saintly and venerable hands. And then he fell asleep in the Lord. And already the one who came after him was journeying toward

---

* Matt. 16:19
** Acts 12:7, 8
*** 2 Peter 3:8

Jerusalem to meet the eastern Patriarch, and the star that guided them stopped above the garden of Gethsemane where the Lord was betrayed by a kiss.

Peter has seen again the lake where he abandoned his boat and nets to become a fisher of men. What have his nets brought back during the nineteen centuries that he has cast them into the human sea? Has he perhaps thought of the time when he wanted to dominate all the kingdoms of the world, when what he received freely he did not give freely—and of the times when he could not prevent Christian princes from using basely the name of Christ? The proclaiming of the Good News served as pretext for ruthless conquests. The Gospel, for entire races of men, became the synonym for servitude and destruction.

I imagine Simon-Peter weeping, as he wept on the night of the Passion, in the courtyard of the High Priest. The crowing of the cock transfixed the cold dawn. The servants and the soldiers had drawn near the dying fire. Jesus, who had by then been spat upon and buffeted, passed nearby, his hands bound, and looked at Peter. It was then that Peter "went out, and wept bitterly."*

And now the Lord God is exhorting Simon-Peter to console himself and rejoice, because the Christian mystery always comes down to this never-ending defeat which is its triumph: the Son of Man, nailed to a gallows in the very center of the human tragedy, has divided the history of the world into two parts—and He remains more living than any living person and more beloved. And it is true that in Jerusalem there are still Jews who refused to recognize Him, and the sons of Ishmael are likewise there, and they followed another prophet. "But know ye not," said the Lord, "that a little leaven leaveneth the whole lump?"**

Can it be that the Holy Father had one single moment of solitude for that encounter with the Lord? In order to have it, he would have needed, at the decline of the day, to advance alone on the road that leads from Jerusalem to Emmaus. Then Someone would have walked beside him, and without uttering a single word

---

* Matt. 26:75
** 1 Cor. 5:6

would have been recognized. And the Holy Father would at last have received a sign, and we too, through him. But no, we do not demand a sign. We demand no other sign than the accomplishments in Holy Church at the present period of history. An old Catholic such as I am, born toward the end of the last century, could not have imagined ever having the joy of hearing, before sinking into eternal sleep, that tramping of the flocks of all the sheepfolds, those bleatings, those clarions of bells surrounding Simon-Peter as he came from Rome to Jerusalem. His meeting with the Patriarch of the east beside the empty sepulchre calls to mind the enigmatic words of the Lord: "For wheresoever the carcass is, there will the eagles be gathered together."* But one should say, there where the body no longer is and has not been since the night of the Resurrection. And the assembled eagles will be not only Christians of all rites, but Israel will also be represented, and the sons of Ishmael, those enemy brothers, since the Jews, like ourselves, are issued from Abraham and are therefore blessed in the Messiah who was to come and who did come. What all the nations of the earth foresee today is that the pilgrimage of Pope Paul VI to Jerusalem gives the signal, beyond race and beyond all confessions of the faith, for the first great assembly of the human family.

And now I have only to let myself be borne along to the eternal life by that flood of the holy Liturgy. I no longer know what year it is nor what my age is, but I know that we are approaching Christmas.

For seventy years, now, the candles of the crèche no longer light that corner of a dark and freezing cold bedroom adjoining my grandmother's room, which we never entered except on the eve of Noël. The ritual emotion arises in me without an effort. Mentally I can still smell those blue candles which we extinguished—after disputing the privilege—restoring the room to darkness. An old chronicler knows what he will find in the drawer labeled *Noël*, if he goes to the trouble of rummaging there.

With this as starting point I could add my reasons to those that have put off my younger fellow-writers from a certain literary

---

* Matt. 24:28

flourish that has made them loathe "fine writing" and rendered suspect anything the least inflated. What makes Sartre despise "pure souls" is the falsification of sentiments on which a certain literature has subsisted, especially since Jean-Jacques Rousseau. The noble style of Chateaubriand magnificently suits that fabrication. Who among us can declare himself without sin in this respect? We have been guilty of it at times, even I, who have been immunized from my earliest years by the antidote of Pascal and Racine.

And yet . . . I am not being untruthful when I say that I believe in the soul, in my soul, and thus in the soul of every human being. I am not playing with words when I write "Grace" for the love it signifies. And in spite of any of the advantageous attitudes we might assume quite naturally since they have become second nature, the true and the real are what that literature exploits and deforms:

> *Elle dit, la voix reconnue,*
> *Que la bonté c'est notre vie . . .*

Yes, the familiar voice says that goodness is our life. Reality, no matter how we define it, is the truth from which proceeds all poetry. Can we all have been deceived when we believed it could be attained beyond things, objects? And which of the two has significance, the object, or the individual who observes it and is conscious of it? One might dwell on that word "conscious" and its implications. One could put it in parentheses, but one cannot suppress it. Can we have been liars, we who have not thrown overboard what we discovered deep within us?

We have been liars if we have pretended not to know what is bad and what is good, and if this knowledge has not been linked with a love from which we find ourselves separated when we do wrong. But that love is restored to us at any moment; we need but pronounce a name in a certain tone of voice.

It is not for us to judge our accomplishments. But we can attest to the reality of what we have described. To conclude that there is nothing beyond the visible object, or at least nothing that we can apprehend, is one of the gravest falsifications we could be guilty of making, we writers with our fine style and our fine sentiments.

"To take up a favorite piece of academical criticism," wrote Alain Robbe-Grillet recently, "Roussel is blamed for not having *something to say . . ."* And because of this very lacking of something to say, Robbe-Grillet thinks Roussel is admirable. To confuse "something to say" with dusty academical criticism is not, with certain writers of today, as it was in the time of the Dadaists and the first surrealists, an attempt at spiritual emancipation carried out by young rebels. Moreover, they are no longer so young. As strict logicians they draw the consequences from the premises laid down at the beginning. And in fact, from one point of view, we will give them the credit of being truly innovators. Before them, who, either close to us or as far back as we can go, what writer did not have something to say? They did not all have the same things to say, but within a body of work something was said. Beauty could spring from the anguish of contradiction: for example, Rimbaud, or Baudelaire.

The ebb-tide has carried me so far from those writers who emphasize the object and deny the spirit, that they have little importance for me. I care not a fig for them. But this is not a literary debate; it is an inner and spiritual debate. It takes place in the minds of people, not in books and periodicals. It is in the latter that we see proclaimed the triumph of "nothing" over "something"—that something which is everything to me. This superiority complex in those writers who have thrown overboard the last hope of man no longer irritates me as formerly, but there are times when I could weep over it "because love is no longer loved," as a certain saint put it. Formerly I put my trust in other writers, such as Claudel, and Bernanos. I talked with Du Bos, I talked with Maritain. And even though we met but rarely, I knew they were somewhere on earth, working and praying. I was not alone.

One would say that God no longer needs men of letters. This is what finally happens when men of letters have believed they no longer need God.

However, the history of mankind, which you new writers refuse to depict or interpret or transpose, continues to unfold. You can go off into a corner and play knucklebones if you like, while the most powerful poem is being manifested in the Vatican. The tragedy looking for a tragic subject, why, it may be found in the life and death of President Kennedy. You who can find amusement only in your game of knucklebones, please realize that the subjects—the "objects"—of Shakespeare and Balzac and Tolstoy remain, and after all there is no need of an audience to attend the tragedy you will never write.

There is likewise the human face, just as the little screen of the television shows me; it exists, but painters of today refuse to see it any more. Nonetheless, it is there and nothing is more strange, more unknown in the world; it is still the unique enigma worth solving. And all the rest, all that you call literature and painting, has become what interests me no more.

What does interest me, still? I question myself upon returning from an early Mass where I did not hear the angels sing—or rather, where I heard them weep, if angels weep. You see, for an old man it is hard to distinguish between Christmas and All Saints Day; the bells within him ring out from the depths of a night which is both that of lost childhood and eternity beginning. And lo, he has already become dust—a dust irresistibly sucked into that infinite void which has engulfed one by one his grandparents, his mother, his three brothers, the friends he most loved, almost all of them departed at the dawn of their life and his life, while he remains alone to revive the already almost obliterated visage. What sound had their voices? Can we hear those voices again that sounded before they could be recorded? That particular accent, that particular laugh of Philippe, of Jean, of Raymond . . .

The old man clasps his arms around the void . . . And now he feels against him the warmth of a small body he brought home from that early Mass, that Child he carried, wrapped in his cloak. An illusion? Why, no. Those he loved are living. And I'm aware that it is too little to say that I believe it; I know it, thanks to that infant. It is of less importance to me to believe that this dust will resuscitate than to know that every one of those souls is living now, and seeing me. And if it seems insane to imagine that those thousands of millions of beings that perished go on living forever, it is because we find it difficult to escape time, space, number, and because we cannot conceive the absolute worth to God of a single human soul. And when I recall such and such a one of those who have fallen into their last sleep, what strikes me is the absolute singularity of each soul, the uniqueness of each individual, making him a world to himself, more circumscribed than any planet in the teeming milky way of souls, a thinking, loving, and deserving world.

True, an anxious part of me is constantly repeating the question Nicodemus put to Christ: "How can these things be?"* No other response is given except that peace which rises from an early Mass begun in tears. The peace of Christmas rejoins the peace of the Resurrection, the peace of Pentecost—it is the same as is the bread broken on those days among so many millions of human beings—the same bread—miracle of a multiplication that has endured for nineteen centuries.

I restore the mystery of Christmas to its essentials, excluding the accretions of the legendary or figurative which have overloaded it: that infant God, the infant I press against me as did the aged Simeon in the temple, already wounded in feet and hands. In advance we have taken Him down from the cross, and if He is within us this morning as in other mornings, it is because He is already resurrected. He has given us in advance the peace of Christmas, for this is what He was to promise to His followers during His last night on earth: "Peace I leave with you, my peace I give unto you: not as the world giveth, give I unto you . . ."**

Such was my meditation this Christmas . . . Is this all that interests me, still, only this? It is all too true that old age, even when it does not show itself in an enfeeblement of the mind, does not in the least escape a progressive diminishing of the interest we once took in things, finally including everything called passion (in both the sense of love and the sense of suffering). I can no longer tolerate being involved in that eternal story of the human couple projected on the silver screen. I also, at the same time, avoid the possibilities of nostalgia and disgust. And above all, I fear being bored.

Some of my friends are surprised that I could have agreed to write a weekly television chronicle—and indeed, I was often on the point of giving it up. But to do so would have been to shut the last small window opening upon the agitations of the present time. I no longer go to the cinema, but snatches of films writhe for an instant

---

* John 3:9
** John 14:27

on the small television screen, like bacilli in a laboratory test tube, and it is truly the bacilli of the evil I survive. Crowds fill the stadiums where I go no more—but did I ever enter them? And here, my fellow-men, are some distinguished writers who have come to talk about their books, who believe in their own importance as I once believed in mine; here are some actors who are trying to be simple and natural but are doomed never to be, for they will play parts to the very end and will be true to themselves for the first and only time on their deathbeds.

All this the television gave me at the cost of one hour of attention. And then I pressed a button and withdrew into my silence, into that peace I spoke about, which concerns only me. But what about politics? Oh, yes, that is the strange thing: politics do not divert me from my peace. Yet what could there be that is apparently more opposite to the eternal than that mess of errors and violence? However, although this is a poor epoch in literature, it is a very great political epoch. No one today really dominates the literature of the newcomers (for Sartre, and we are struck by this when we read what he has just written about his childhood in his magazine, *Les Temps Modernes*, is the last writer of our generation and not the forerunner of those who came after him. He is closer to Proust in those pages, the poetic portions at least, than to Robbe-Grillet). No one after him seems to dominate literary history. On the other hand, in history itself, this is the epoch of individuals. We have seen what was accomplished in Rome by the most disarmed and feeble old man during the brief papacy of John XXIII, and the same spirit has made of his successor Paul VI a humble man who at last seeks and finds in Bethlehem and Nazareth the traces of that God without *sedia* or *tiara* or *flabelli*—although that God he found had also been elevated above the earth, but nailed there.

The Nile of the liturgy continues to bear me, this old man, from one communion to another . . .

This sudden fading of the world may be due to the absence of sunshine, but also, I imagine, to the bile in me, some earthly nourishment that is hard to digest. Our melancholy, our anxiety which we attribute to more elevated causes, we are sufficiently humble to concede that it is almost always, in part, physiological.

But there is a direct cause for my disenchantment; silence has been murdered. There is no longer silence anywhere. On the old estates where the birds do not nest in as great a number as before, invisible lunatics penetrate the sound barrier. The walls that resisted the centuries now tremble to their foundations, doors sag, sometimes ceilings crack. When the wind blows from the south, it brings us the clamor of engines, and a cement-breaker nearby. This valley of the Garonne, bordered by the long line of forest, no longer evokes for me as it did in my childhood the verse I loved in *La Maison du berger:* "The vast silent countryside stretching away and away . . ." The plain is no longer silent. And I have lost the power I once had of embellishing the things and people here. I renounce my hitherto continuous effort to reinvent, in order to maintain the world at the level of my dreams.

The minute I stop meddling, this bitter springtime must not be counted on to conceal the leprous condition of the decrepit walls, for the Virginia creeper does not yet have leaves, and in the moribund linden-trees the balls of mistletoe that I was unable to destroy are vegetable tumors. We writers believe we are the agents and servants of the world's orchestration. Well, suddenly I feel I have had enough of it. The engine rules the earth and sky. Chemistry poisons the birds, and certain species disappear. The nightingale—shall I hear it sing this summer, that bird which kept me from sleeping in former times?

The world (the appearance of the world) leaves us before we leave it, effacing itself so that we remain alone, not with ourselves, but with Him who is in us.

This is the subject of my meditation during these first days of Holy Week. The better part of my being, that of the writer, will have been completely open toward the world; it will have been literally under the spell of a familiar aspect of my native countryside, without my having ever yielded to curiosity about other horizons; in short, I, whom some people regard as a master of the inner life, shall have been all my life long "beside myself," glued to appearances, like a poor fly on fly-paper.

Now that the outside world betrays me and becomes unbreatheable, it is time to put into practice what has so often been the subject of my writings and remind myself that the Kingdom of God is within us.

Christ will enter into His agony tomorrow evening, which is

Holy Thursday; He must have loved that garden to which He often went with His followers, as I love the garden where I am writing at this moment. That garden was for Him a place of rest, of fellowship, of meditation, perhaps. And now, in the interval of one night, all the suffering of the world was to be contained: the silence of the Father, the sleeping of His friends, then their forsaking Him after the betrayal by the kiss, the first outrages, the denial.

This fading of the world which makes me suffer may at least help me to put up with nature, no more as an enchantment but as a theatre indifferent to the drama that is unfolding—like the place of which Pascal wrote: "Jesus is in a garden, not of delights as was the first Adam, but of torments . . ." But in truth I am not in such a garden. My garden is merely disenchanted, the disenchantment being a torment within my powers of endurance.

That power I had of embellishing an ingrate land and to orchestrate my poor life is now lost, and sometimes the loss extends to religious matters. In the garden which is no longer a garden of delights, what remains of the Father, if I suppress everything that crystallizes in me around the effusions of religion which perhaps originated nowhere but within me? That thought helps me enter into the worst moment of Christ's agony, when He cried out, "My God, my God, why hast thou forsaken me?"*

But I must beware! In this night before Holy Thursday in the disenchanted garden, I must not yield to a somber inclination. To darken is another way of embellishing and searching for some morbid delectation.

In thought I leave the garden. I go away with Simon-Peter. Behind him, I enter into the courtyard of the High Priest. I sit down near the fire the soldiers and servants have lit on this chilly night of spring. I hold out my hands to the flame. I reply to the questions asked, but I reply with the words Simon-Peter wished he had said and did not say: "Yes, I too was with that man; yes, I was with Him from the beginning. Yes, I know that man you mention."

I have nothing more to do than to give that reply, and to wait, holding my old hands out to the fire.

---

* Matt. 27:46

About the Author . . .

François Mauriac, poet, critic, biographer and novelist, was born in Bordeaux, France, on October 11, 1885. Unlike his father, who had some talent for writing and a love for books but died a banker, Mauriac made the decision early in his life to devote himself to literature.

In 1905 he received his Master of Arts degree in Bordeaux and the next year arrived in Paris to study for the École des Chartres examinations. It was there that his long career was launched. A collection of his poetry, *Les Mains Jointes*, was published in 1909 and came to the favorable attention of the influential Maurice Barrès. Mauriac became part of the literary group that founded the Catholic periodical *Les Cahiers*. A second book of poetry, *L'Adieu à l'Adolescence*, appeared in 1911, followed in 1913 by his first novel, *L'Enfant chargé de Chaines*. That same year, 1913, Mauriac was married to Jeanne Lafon. The marriage produced four children, Claire, Luce, Claude (novelist and critic), and Jean.

His second novel, *La Robe prétexte*, was published in 1914. With the coming of World War I, Mauriac enlisted in an ambulance corps, but he contracted a fever which hospitalized him and removed him from the fighting.

His work continued: *La Chair et le Sang*, published in 1920, and *Préséances* in 1921. For a time Mauriac was drama critic for the important monthly *N.R.F.* (*Nouvelle Revue Française*).

But it was not until 1922, with the publication of *Le baiser au lépreux* (The Kiss of the Leper), that Mauriac won a large public. From 1922 until his operation in 1932, he produced short stories, essays and a series of novels: *Genitrix, Le mal, Le désert de l'amour, Thérèse Desqueyroux, Destins* and *Ce qui était perdu*. *Genitrix* and *Le baiser au lépreux* won for him the Grand Prix du Roman in 1925. Finally, in 1933, he was elected to the French Academy.

François Mauriac has always been a force in French political life through his writings. During the Spanish Civil War he opposed Franco. Later on, detesting Vichy and the German Occupation, he participated in the literary Resistance and wrote for the clandestine publishers, "Les Editions de Minuit," *Le Cahier Noir*, which expressed his feelings during those troubled years, using of necessity the pseudonym *Forez*. This book was published in 1943, one year before the liberation of Paris. During this period he also contributed to liberal-Catholic magazines *Sept* and *Temps Présent*. Mauriac has never lacked moral courage.

Yet the war did not divert the main body of his work. *La Pharisienne* appeared in 1941, and a play, *Asmodée*, won great success on the eve of the war. Although Mauriac does not consider himself a writer for the theatre, two of his plays, *Asmodée* and *Les mal aimés*, are still in the repertory of the Comédie Française. After the war, Mauriac produced many essays, along with *Le Sagouin*, *Le feu sur la terre*, *Galigaï* and, in 1954, *L'Agneau*.

In 1952 François Mauriac was awarded the Nobel Prize in Literature.

François Mauriac probes in his work the life of the French provincial family, the bourgeois milieu of his own childhood. In his memoirs he immerses himself in that childhood of fragrant kitchens, Catholic holy days, changing seasons, bachelor uncles, all-powerful women guarding the family patrimony, the schoolroom that took him away from his mother, and, finally, those blissfully happy summer holidays. He came out of that milieu a dedicated writer and a devout Christian. For Mauriac Christianity is neither theology nor philosophy, but a "really true story" to be told and retold like a child's fondest tale—a constant revelation.

DATE DUE

A